Anxiety Mindset Diaries

Don't Let Go

Through Post-Traumatic-Stress as a Mind Coach

JO HARRIS

Jot The Thought Media Ltd

JOT THE THOUGHT

For permissions requests, write to the publisher at the address below:
Jot The Thought Media Ltd.
Suite 519, 800-15355 24th Avenue
Surrey, BC, V4A 2H9
Canada   Email: hello@jotthethought.com

Cover design by Jo Harris, Interior Design Jo Harris, Cover Photo courtesy of the Author, Images and Art created under license by Canva.com, DALL-E

1st Edition Printed in Canada
PAPERBACK ISBN: 978-1-0689057-3-5
HARDCOVER ISBN: 978-1-0689057-4-2
E-BOOK ISBN: 978-1-0689057-1-1
AUDIO BOOK ISBN: 978-1-0689057-2-8

This book is for anyone!

From my spirit to your spirit!

Table of Contents

Introduction

Anxiety Mindset Diaries - Navigating PTSD: A Coach's Journey of Insight and Resilience

In Anxiety Mindset Diaries readers/listeners embark on a journey through the landscape of Post-Traumatic Stress Disorder (PTSD), by the unique perspective of a mind coach who has traversed the challenging terrains of PTSD personally. This book is structured to serve not only as a beacon of understanding but also as a source of solace and empowerment for those affected by PTSD and their supporters. Each chapter of the book is intentionally divided into two distinct but complementary sections:

1. **Informational Insight**: The first section of every chapter delves into various aspects of PTSD, with a special focus on phenomena such as heightened anxiety. Here, readers will find careful articulation detailing the many facets of PTSD. This part aims to enlighten the audience about the complexities, while demystifying the condition and providing a solid foundation of understanding.

2. **Personal Reflections**: In the second part, the book takes a deeply personal turn. Drawing from my own journey through PTSD, I share my thoughts, feelings, and experiences related to the chapter's topic. This narrative is not just a recounting of events; it's an intimate exploration of the emotional and psychological landscape I navigated. Through these reflections, I aim to connect with readers on a personal and emotional level, offering insight into the inner workings of a mind grappling with PTSD, and illustrating how resilience, understanding, and compassion can illuminate the path to healing.

Anxiety Mindset Diaries is more than a book; it's a companion for those seeking to understand PTSD from both a clinical and a deeply personal viewpoint. It's crafted for individuals navigating their own journey with PTSD, for loved ones seeking to support them, and for professionals desiring to enrich their understanding of this complex condition. By weaving together professional insights with personal narratives, in hopes of fostering a compassionate, comprehensive understanding of PTSD, encouraging a mindset where healing is seen as a journey rather than a destination.

WITH PURPOSE

In recent years, there has been a significant increase in discussions surrounding mental health and wellness. The importance of understanding, supporting, and prioritizing our mental well-being has become a prevalent topic in various platforms and conversations. However, despite the progress made, it is disheartening to realize that a negative stigma persists around mental health. Feeling stressed out or showing anxiety in some manner is real and happens to almost everyone in some manner.

This stigma acts as a barrier, preventing many individuals from seeking the help they need or even acknowledging their struggles. It perpetuates misconceptions, fear, and judgment, ultimately hindering the progress of those on their mental health journeys. It is essential that we strive to eradicate this stigma and expand our compassion not only towards others but also towards ourselves.

Each person's mental journey is unique, and it requires a compassionate and open-minded approach to truly support and understand one another. Advocacy for mental health should encompass all individuals, regardless of gender or age. Women, men, children, and everyone in between deserve empathy, care, and support in their pursuit of well-being.

Let us promote an environment of acceptance and understanding where seeking help is seen as a sign of strength, not weakness. By advocating for mental health with open hearts and minds, we can break down the barriers that prevent people from accessing the support they need. Together, we can foster a society that values mental health as an integral part of overall well-being, ensuring that no one is left to face their challenges alone.

In three words I can sum up everything I've learned about life.

It goes on!

~ROBERT FROST

My Story

Falling off the Bike

Yup! This is me around three years old losing control and letting go of the handlebars while riding my bike! My face here is a perfect example of how we all have felt, perhaps a few times in our lives.

I feel the picture is so symbolic of what I experienced, and the feelings experienced when feeling out of control emotionally and mentally. My journey was from a place of being in control and never letting go of the handlebars, metaphorically. However, there came sudden and profound experiences that shattered my sense of control, plunging me into a state of intense fear and anxiety. Shocking me so deeply that I felt I was losing my soul and desire to exist.

Thankfully my soul survived and pulled me up, and through the darkest times of my life, back to a happier and healthier me.
Let me share with you, my story!

My Post Traumatic Stress journey lasted not just for a few months or a year, but for a profound three years. This experience has granted me a deeper appreciation for clients and anyone who has battled deep anxiety for great lengths of time. However, time is irrelevant as "heightened anxiety" can feel like decades. It takes an immense amount of effort and perseverance to transform the energy within your body and mind. While I always empathized with these struggles for others, it wasn't until I experienced it myself to such an intense degree that I truly comprehended the magnitude of the pain emotionally, mentally, and physically endured.

During this time, events occurred that took me to a place I had never been before. For the first time in my entire life, I found myself grappling with suicidal thoughts. It was a frightening and eye-opening experience that allowed me to truly understand why someone might reach such a despairing point. In the past, I could empathize with those struggling, but I couldn't fully grasp the depths of their anguish. Now, however, I possess both compassion and genuine understanding for individuals who have experienced those dark thoughts.

I often found myself feeling isolated and hesitant to reach out for support, as I had always been in the role of a coach and mentor. Unfortunately, I also encountered a disheartening lack of empathy or care from individuals who presented themselves as advocates for well-being and tote the empowerment of women, women helping women. Something that shocked me. However, these experiences have only fueled my commitment to fostering genuine empathy and understanding, and I have renewed my dedication to advocating for the mental health and wellness of all individuals.

I believe that everyone deserves access to compassionate care and support, regardless of their background or circumstances. I am motivated to create positive change, both in my work and in the broader community, to ensure that no one feels alone or unsupported on their journey toward well-being.

This book reaches out to all who find themselves wrestling with the shadows of heightened anxiety—whether you're struggling with this yourself or standing alongside someone who is and striving to comprehend it. I hope that sharing my own journey will inspire hope and offer a beacon of light to guide you through the complexity of anxiety. May this journey spark a deeper understanding, compassion, and kindness within you.

Unravelled

Navigating the abyss of fear and anxiety as mind coach

"I didn't really have much issue with being vulnerable except perhaps crying in front of people. Whatever happened to me during the 3 years of Post Traumatic Stress, made me feel so vulnerable I was like a frozen rabbit approaching everything in my life including my family."

How the hell did this happen to me? Is always hovering in the back of my mind like a popcorn kernel stuck in your tooth. You know the ones that slide in and out of the gum under a tooth that you just can't seem to get out for days. And it is painful periodically. This is truly how I feel about that question, hopefully it finally just pops out and disappears one day.

My life is full of circumstances, situations, people and events that were to say the least, not ok, shitty and some even life threatening. None of them left me traumatized or feeling victimized. I could always pull through and see ways to grow. They all contributed to the person I became. I became strong and quite capable of dealing with life. I also was able to keep the openhearted, caring, compassionate, and optimistic part of me alive.

My life and how I managed to get through the many rattling events was a key component to why I was successful as a mind coach and hypnotherapist. It was something that just was natural for me.

The events that happened the end of 2020 and onward unravelled every thread of strength, hope, trust and endurance I ever held. They ripped me wide open and left me vulnerable for repeat injury. Like a scared rabbit sitting in an empty swimming pool surround by hungry wolves with no where to escape.

That is how I subconsciously felt, and that anchor of terror rose like beast excited to consume me. Consume me? It did, to the point I began to have the desire not to live anymore. The pain, the anguish, the fear, the doubts they became a bonfire raging out of control inside of me. I lost all the ability to navigate mentally, emotionally out of it like I had done over and over throughout my life.

I have no idea if this is how others have felt during PTSD, but I felt like I was drugged, it felt like I was experiencing things and hallucinating on and off and together at times, and I have no idea why. Other than that is my perspective of what it felt like to lose complete control and be terrified. Unravelled to the core literally. The worst part is inside of that I also felt embarrassed, deeply embarrassed for the first time in my life. Why? Because my strength and ability is what made me a good coach for so many years and good ear for so many others throughout my life. And because this was not who I was.

So, who was I now?

A complete fucking mess, drowning and suffocating from the limitless weight of the thoughts, emotions and feelings. Looking through a straw the size of they eye of tiny sewing needle, impossible to thread, trying to see the flickering light to hold onto.

I will say this a lot moving forward, because it is simply just true. Just don't let go!

Here I will share my thoughts, perspectives and truths about what I see is necessary to help those through PTSD or any level of heightened anxiety and what I experienced and perceived at the time. They are my interpretations, they are not researched other than the Part One: What is PTSD, I researched that and discovered I had 17 of the above 19 symptoms.

So, here we are, because I made it through.

Please note: The "personal perspectives" in this book have mostly been transcribed from raw dictation recordings, therefore, the audio version of this book is narrated by me and will likely give a different perspective with the sound of emotions in my voice as I did not edit that out. I felt it important for the listener to experience the feelings.

Journaling Notes

Insights of real moments captured.

The next 4 entries are a glimpse of my journaling notes, raw insight to the thoughts and feelings I experienced.
Real moments.
They are unedited, difficult to share, but important factual representations in snippets throughout this difficult time of heightened anxiety for me.

*****Explicit language will and may apply.
I apologize.

Entry One: Losing My Soul

Every day I ask myself why? And then, what do I want? What do I do? I can't find the answer. I've always been someone who has stopped and looked from the outside in when I've been in certain situations or emotional situations, even conflict. Now when I do this, I'm lost. I see it. I look at it, I feel it, and then I go blank.
It has been one of the most difficult things of the healing process to watch myself do and know how to change it.

The memories of working with clients, the rewarding feelings from helping others, and the memory of who I was before hits gives me some semblance of hope that I can find my way back, but it's like a dangling string, more like a spider web thread that I can barely grab a hold of or see. I keep trying to focus on gaining that back because I know somewhere inside, it was the strongest part of me.

Somewhere in the middle of all of this, probably for the 25th, 20th, Or 100th time of hurting my husband's heart, I told him I felt like I was losing my soul. I believe that was shocking to him, and he had no idea how to handle that. I'm not sure I would have either, if someone said that to me.

What does that mean? for me, it means I feel stiff. I feel blank. I feel emotionally cold a lot. It is almost like I don't feel then, every once in a while, I feel again. Is this damage or is this self protection? During the darkest times I felt fear and terror so extreme it was unbearable.

This is very likely the contributing factor to the thoughts of just dying. Actually, it is in the blank **feelingless** moments, these thoughts come. Then no connection of meaning for anything to do with me. In other words, I can't find meaning.

Then the old me that somehow cracks through and stops and looks, thankfully, where I have a moment of feeling, "No, this is not true", and you would never feel this way, why do you now? I still don't really understand or have a good answer for that. Except perhaps that I am in a seesaw of having spirit and losing spirit.

Losing the connection to my soul. This is a scary thing to watch from the outside looking in. That is how it feels. You can't jump start the emotions back to life.

Yesterday I had joy for five or 10 minutes playing with my dogs. Then again, when one decided they needed to come and give love and licks and kisses, then the other had to join in.

You must know, I burst into tears as I take the time to write this. I realized how much joy I felt in those precious moments. And how rare it is for me.

Wohhhh......

I want this part of me back fully and completely. I don't believe I would be here today in my healing and striving to get back the happier, healthier me if I did not have my two dogs. Animals have a way of being there without any negative influence. We don't perceive their actions, language or expressions with all of the subconscious negative stories we do as humans.

My two fur babies. Well, four. I had two cats also. Sadly, one is now gone. They are the only things alive, that I did not feel afraid of at some point during that dark time.

My husband, bless his soul, has tried to make me laugh. I love him for the effort.

I realize now that the trying was a roadblock for me and the natural moments of laughter that just occurred for whatever reason are the ones that also brought me that feeling of joy to hold on to. It is sad because in the past, if we were to try to be goofy and make me laugh, I would bend to it and be a goof back and share the love and joy with him.

I'm sure he misses this part of me.

I'm still trying to get back there.

Entry Two: I woke up Ok But Now I am Not

(this is transcribed from the actual voice recording I made, I found it easier sometimes to just hit record and blurt out what I had to)

So, what do you do? I don't know. How do I start? Here's my day.

Realization!!

It's a day where I wake up and I feel OK and I'm not thinking too much, I don't feel like I'm drowning or being pulled down into some sadness. This is not one of those days.

I woke up OK, but now the sun, then not. Maybe it's the rain, or maybe it's the random thought.

Or maybe it's a random post on Facebook that pushed me into "what the fuck?" direction. And brings up memories, painful memories or painful thoughts and feelings. All of the above.

So now here I am. It's 8:07 in the morning and I can already feel the long day where I almost feel like crying already.

Maybe that's what I need to do again is cry and cry.

It's an awful, awful, awful, awful thing to experience on a daily basis. This feeling that everyone around you knows something about what happened to you, and no one will tell you anything.

Straight faced, its all-indirect things and inferences. And they're not nice. They're cruel.

Because they only leave me questioning and wondering what am I supposed to be paying attention to? What am I not?

Am I Fucking crazy?

How could I have gone crazy? Overnight? It's not possible.

Unless I was drugged, then I'm grappling, to find me, the strong me, that would just say fuck this shit and put her fucking shoes on and walk out the door and look at everybody like kiss my Ass!!

But it's a really awful thing. To not be able to do that, to feel scared. When am I safe? Am I actually safe? Was I ever safe?

What am I afraid of? What do I need to be afraid of?

Maybe it's just me. That's an awful feeling in itself, that sometimes is perhaps more debilitating to even consider.

This is what happens to your brain. When people mess with it?

And then you're, left messing with it, trying to you find your way back trying to just be strong, clear, focused.

These mornings are the hardest ones, because I cannot make a decision, and no one understands. No one can even come close to understanding because they don't feel what I feel.

It's like people having pain or debilitating pain. People don't believe they are in pain because they can't see the gaping gash bleeding and grossing them out. We're so insensitive to what we can't see, but sometimes what we can't see is actually worse. It's the unknown why? Deeper, it's darker.

It cuts inside out.

And how do you heal the inside from the outside when you can't even get to it?

Without cutting you open.

I don't even know what to say. Sometimes I try every day to find the one or two or three questions that are so spot on that I can ask that will produce something for me that I need.

But I guess it's figuring out what do I really need to be able to find those questions, and I'm not even sure what I really need.

I feel for every single soul on this planet that feels alone, because even though I'm not entirely alone, I feel so fucking alone.

And I've never felt that way in my entire fucking life. Never. Not once. And it's fucking debilitating. No one has any understanding other than people who really feel it. I feel for you, I swear to God I feel for you.

And I wish I could reach out and hold each and every one of your hands, and say it's going to be OK. (crying)

uhhhhhh

OK. That's all I can handle. I think I'll go too far down the fucking hole of sadness.

Why is that open?

Seven fucking minutes. Yeah, that's great. I can only handle 7 minutes!

Entry three: Ramblings, (You Can Be Broken)

(this is transcribed from the actual voice recording I made, I found it easier sometimes to just hit record and blurt out what I had to)

PS: it is a wee bit messy as I role my eyes somewhat embarrassed, but it gives insight, so I freely share with you.

There are people that knew me years ago and if they read this story or get involved in this story in any way, or understand it, they're going to probably be very shocked because in the past I was very candid and open about me, and who I am and what I've been through. I was always honest about my stories, if the opportunity to share that came up for some reason, it was a relevant subject of... I didn't just whine about stuff, because I didn't actually feel like I needed to whine about my past and the things that I had gone through and experienced and overcame.

Because I felt that I was who I was, I was as strong as I was, and I was the person that I was, that everybody, ummm, liked and valued and I felt good about who I was and where I was and how I treated people and how I cared about people and, and myself even, probably sometimes didn't care about myself enough. But you know, we all do that.

Anyways. I never really complained.
People go, Oh my God, I can't believe you went through that and I'd be like, no, It's ok, you know, like sometimes life teaches you things and it opens you up to be either aware or not aware. And I feel that I am who I am because of everything that I've gone through, and it doesn't really affect me. It's just an acceptance that has occurred.

And, I know, I know I don't currently have the right to whine and complain because there's really people out there that are going through far, far, far worse. And there always will be, no matter who we are, I guess. And what the journey is that we go on.

When life attacked us, my family, my husband and I, me, I don't even know entirely at this moment, what the attack originated to, for who?

When that occurred and it unraveled and ummm...During COVID, which was also a world dominating PTSD experience for every freaking body, and I think people are still healing from that.

Never mind whatever sad, debilitating stories occurrences that happened during that time for them............which is similar to what happened to us, and we felt literally attacked and um it just got worse, and worse. And watching it from the inside was horrific. I can't even tell you there are no words to share the pain physically and mentally, emotionally and coming out of it and looking at it, there still are no words to share the pain physically, mentally, emotionally.

And, and I don't feel entirely the same as I did before. I don't feel as strong as I was before, even though I know that's the person who I really am. I've been battling and struggling to access that same strength, and it's a horrible experience.

So, I sit today saying. (crying)

It sucks, because you can be broken. Literally broken, and shattered, and struggle, and feel completely lost and alone.

But you can fight, scratch and claw your way back. I guarantee you. You can, and even today, as I talk about this, and I cry because that's the person I am. I just am very emotional about life and feelings, and when I talk about this, I talk about it for everyone else, not for me. It's really not for me, even though I need, needed to talk to somebody to vent. And I didn't have anybody to vent to because I had no idea who to trust.

And that's a really horrible feeling. And I know that, you know, over the years, my clients felt probably that way. How do you find a therapist or a coach or a mentor or somebody to talk to you that you can literally trust with the deepest secrets, thoughts that you're having? You know, it's tough. It's really tough.

So, this is a journey for everybody. A journey of I don't want to call it mental health because mental health has become such a used and abused statement, not even a statement, two words that people are using one way, and using another way, and now how do you even trust that. It's more of a mind journey? It's just a mental journey and life is literally one big ass mental journey of finding yourself and finding grounding and finding strength and finding....Finding a deeper sense of truth, and I don't believe the deeper sense of truth is, ahhh fluffy and puffy and, you know, flowers and trees. I think that people and humans are here to figure out how to exist and coexist with the life on this planet that is unbelievably profound.

I mean the life as to the trees, the bees, the animals, the oceans, the mountains, everything that you name it, that the entire planet and everything else other than humans that exist, we are actually meant to figure out how to coexist with them and each other.

In a respectable way, not selfish, not self centred, not greedy. Not. I'm going to be the best or the king or the queen. Just I'm going to be really good.

Wouldn't that be an amazing place? If the world could actually go there, if we all, each and every single person here could actually just go there.

That's what this journey and my journey and telling the story and everything I want to talk about will probably always go up and down and around, and back to that, because it's essentially the reason that we went through what we went through because people didn't care, I don't know.

__Reflecting on this entry -3 years later:__ I see how I was trying to find a way to talk to myself. To remind myself of the strength and good parts of me that were still there. This was crazy hard for me to listen to, as it sounds awful with babbling incoherent sentences. Honestly if I didn't know better, I would say drunk LOL, but I was not.

Entry Four: After the Terror Came Rage

Journaling pages summary written October 21st, 2023.

After the terror came volcanic rage.

It was when I was hurt and hurting the most that I felt a beast of rage crawl throughout my veins like red hot lava. I have never in my life felt rage like this. This rage caged my soul, spirit and heart with walls, giving me less understanding and empathy, more of blank emotions in response to everything. Then the sheer burning frustration and rage would burst out in volcanic anger, attempting to release the emotional weight and pressure.

My husband was on the receiving end of this. Unfortunately, more often than fair for him to bare, we've been together for 18 years and until this thing happened to me, we barely fought. I'm amazed he is still by my side. Otherwise, it was the walls in my house, as I burst out yelling to no one but myself.

Some would think this is unhealthy. I disagree. It released little bits of the unknown pressure allowing space inside me for my thoughts, feelings and emotions. Giving me room to breathe and attempt, turning them in a different direction.

I believe it was necessary for the many articulations of anger. To hold it was unhealthy for my body and mind. I can confidently say that the rage I felt was so deep and encompassing, it was infused into every cell of my body, squeezed my breath so tightly shut that I physically and emotionally had no choice but to explode if nothing but to save myself from dying from the constricting pressure.

What did I feel this rage for? Everything. Everyone, and at myself. The rage for everything and everyone was about being victimized and then being left alone.

I am not sure if the awareness of feeling that anger towards myself is from being a victim or the guilt of feeling like a victim, because I have always been able to get through tough times relatively easy and quickly. I do know that some of it is from guilt for emotional outbursts, my thoughts and feelings of doubting and fearing those who I used to feel close to, and trust. And from not knowing or understanding what really happened to me

In the past I was pretty good at finding my breath to calm me down and allow me to think and find a solution to whatever made me upset during these emotional roller coaster years my breath was on a distant vacation with no access, or perhaps it was being held hostage inside the fear, anger, and terror.

I have so many times coached clients to stop and breathe if nothing else, and here I was not able to even think of breathing. I had no access to these thoughts. The only ones that came were the ones that held me prisoner inside myself.

To heal this? Hmm. Not sure what I could say. Not sure that I can say I'm healed. I believe I'm doing better, and better is just that, better.

Every day is a new day. I approach this very differently now as I know each day I wake up lets me know I haven't given up. The day brings hope, even if it feels like a drop instead of a lake full of hope. It is hope that I will find normal again.

So how did I start healing the anger and rage?

I began breaking it down into parts and separating those parts so I could revise, reframe what I was thinking about. Each one of them, when my mind was yelling at everything, feeling like everything was a mess, was gone, changed, damaged, you name it, anything shitty or negative was thrown at that feeling that everything in my life had been destroyed.

And the worst part about this was that it was because of an invisible, unknown attacker that only left me feeling unconsciously responsible for something that I did not do to myself. But I had no solid evidence and no solid way to find out, and no one in my life was taking it as seriously as I was.

It is a very awful thing to be left feeling crazy when those closest to you stay silent and avoid talking with you about how you are. I don't think anyone in my life realizes how alone I felt and how often I still feel alone.

If my dogs could talk, they would have spent all day working through it with me.

I felt their need to be there and to understand if I was OK or not. I would not have made the journey emotionally and mentally back towards myself if I had not seen that need in their eyes, or the safety of knowing they were there for me.

I know one thing when someone tells you they are afraid, you should listen to the why, validate the why as being real to them, and never avoid it or try to distract it. This did not help me at all.

I can safely say that was one of the obstacles to overcome as it contributed to me feeling alone and crazy. But knowing that I was not crazy.

My Deepest Question is Why

My deepest question is why?

Why did I fall right off the Cliff like never before?

The hardest thing for me is the struggle with the thoughts of why? Why! did I fall right off the Cliff?

I've never felt this amount of emotional anxiety, mental fear, physical fear. Not to this degree, ever in my life.

I can't say that enough.

I have had several experiences throughout my life, that were emotional, scary, and difficult. I will share some of them briefly for perspective.

When I was around 7 years old, I had been molested on and off for a few years. When I told my parents, and this man was confronted about what was happening, this man threatened to stick a bottle opener down my throat.

This was also my first experience of feeling protected by a dog, as I was taken to a family friend's home so the family could continue without me there, feeling terrified. These people had a beautiful German shepherd that sat beside me with his head on my lap for four hours.

I will never forget that dog.

This same man threatened to kill me again at the age of 13, as he was now sadly married into my family and he and I had heated words on the phone where I was quite brave to remind him what he had done to me as a child.

My mother, sadly, was struggling all her life with alcoholism and emotional and mental breakdowns. When she was bad, she was bad. Verbally abusive. And when really, really drunk, she could get physical. Sometimes abusive for no good reason other than she was embarrassed.

There were many years of this until I moved out.

She was in serious pain and somehow, I always knew this. Even during the darkest times with her.

In my early 20s, a strange man kicked open my door in the night. Oh yeah, this was shocking and terrifying. At the time, I owned a Wolf Shepherd Cross, and she thankfully was the only reason he never came past that doorway. She was in fierce defence mode. I was holding on to her tightly, and I threatened to let her go if he did not leave. He left and I was OK.

I was stalked twice in my 20s by two different men.

My house was broken into, and I was robbed when I was a single mother in my 30s. That one punched me, in the gut emotionally for about 3 days.

Some of these caused me serious fear at the time, and I overcame them quite quickly, thankfully.

I survived and I used to say I don't regret having these experiences as these things all helped me be the person I am. And I'm strong. I worked through them mentally, emotionally myself, and talking them out.

Throughout my life, I never was afraid to tell my story. I still am not afraid to tell my story at this point. However, I was very afraid to tell my story during these three years of PTSD. I prefer to call it heightened anxiety as I feel this represents the level of maximum anxiety felt.

It was a very different experience altogether. And I was terrified for a number of reasons. This was the worst ingrained feeling, ever! Fear to the core of my body, every bone, every muscle, every cell in my body was vibrating in terror. And I didn't know which way to go. I didn't know which way to turn. I was trying. I was also pretending to be OK. Which was a new experience for me. I kept thinking you're stronger than this, Jo.

It didn't help.

This was the most challenging three years of my life and the worst part about these three years, is that it didn't have to be three years.

Over the first three to four months, I was starting to move through it. Six months later, we ended up moving. We took an opportunity to move to a location that we thought we might think about retiring. And the home was beautiful. We rented a home to test out the location, and to find peace and solace, to heal from the events.

The circumstances turned into a nightmare; I can't even understand that time. I'm still grappling with that, and the type of people that our landlords ended up being. Incapable of responding with empathy and compassion.

The chapter on betrayal and advocate says a little more about this, and about one of them. I thought I could feel safe speaking with them about our situation. I was very wrong. And sadly, those circumstances re-traumatized me in ways I am still having difficulty to explain or understand even.

So, two and a half more years of my life were destroyed thanks to insensitive people.

I see how PTSD can be provoked from past traumas. And even more, when you're in a trauma. Like your body and mind saying, OK, so how many times can I endure this? The past experience can be anchored in the subconscious that are sitting there waiting to be brought back up and used in future events. Where something subconsciously says Nope, I can't take that anymore. Perhaps This is why I broke. I don't know for sure.

I have a difficult time understanding how I was so affected. The situation that happened to me took me off guard. It was three events on top of each other. Two of them, where I was nearly run over by a huge construction truck speeding at warp 9 through my neighborhood while I was out walking the dog. If we were hit by this vehicle, we would have been crushed and thrown the length of two houses, I'm sure.

I felt targeted. There was no proof that I was targeted, of course, and that was difficult. Think train going 80 miles an hour.

Then events that followed around me, they just threw me into a deeper, darker place of fear, I felt stalked. I felt watched. I felt very unsafe. And even in my own home.

I didn't know what was happening, or why it was happening? And if it really had anything to do with me, or if I was just accidentally in it? Until a few things that I experienced, made me believe there was something to what I was feeling, but I couldn't understand why.

The people in my life just brushed it off, so I was alone. And I think that contributed to why I went down and down emotionally. I started to not trust anyone, because no one was listening, and I didn't know what to do. I didn't want to appear crazy and at times I felt crazy. And there was a specific time where, looking at me from the outside, I probably looked crazy or like I was drugged. And believe me, I was not doing drugs of any kind.

But Wow, did it feel like I was drugged with something hallucinogenic. I was not able to gain control of my emotions, my thoughts and the fear. The feelings were so extreme it was like being in a hyper suggestible state. Which in my field is not helpful under these types of circumstances as it is like self hypnotizing the fears and the doubts in, instead of out.

Everything around me pushed every single button of fear and it kept me in that hyper suggestible state. It was awful. It was horrible. It was debilitating. It destroyed my life in so many ways.

Today I'm thankful that I'm still here and I'm able to now take this and share it in hopes of somehow, some way with my story, giving hope to any of you out there with any level of anxiety to that degree. Don't let go.

The light does find its way back in through the cracks.

Just don't let go.

DUAL LENSES: Practical Insights and Personal Reflections on PTSD and Anxiety

1 What is Post Traumatic Stress Dissorder,PTSD

It is natural to feel afraid during and after a traumatic situation. Fear is a part of the body's "fight-or-flight" response, which helps us avoid or respond to potential danger. People may experience a range of reactions after trauma, and most will recover from their symptoms over time. Those who continue to experience symptoms may be diagnosed with post-traumatic stress disorder (PTSD).

Who develops PTSD?

Anyone can develop PTSD at any age. This includes combat veterans and people who have experienced or witnessed a physical or sexual assault, abuse, an accident, a disaster, a terror attack, or other serious events. People who have PTSD may feel stressed or frightened, even when they are no longer in danger.

Not everyone with PTSD has been through a dangerous event. Sometimes, learning that a relative or close friend experienced trauma can cause PTSD.

About 6 of every 100 people will experience PTSD at some point in their lifetime, according to the National Center for PTSD, a U.S. Department of Veterans Affairs program. Women are more likely than men to develop PTSD. Certain aspects of the traumatic event and biological factors (such as genes) may make some people more likely to develop PTSD.

What are the symptoms of PTSD?

Symptoms of PTSD usually begin within 3 months of the traumatic event, but they sometimes emerge later. To meet the criteria for PTSD, a person must have symptoms for longer than 1 month, and the symptoms must be severe enough to interfere with aspects of daily life, such as relationships or work. The symptoms also must be unrelated to medication, substance use, or other illness.

The course of the disorder varies. Although some people recover within 6 months, others have symptoms that last for 1 year or longer. People with PTSD often have co-occurring conditions, such as depression, substance use, or one or more anxiety disorders.

After a dangerous event, it is natural to have some symptoms. For example, some people may feel detached from the experience, as though they are observing things as an outsider rather than experiencing them. A mental health professional—such as a psychiatrist, psychologist, or clinical social worker—can determine whether symptoms meet the criteria for PTSD.

To be diagnosed with PTSD, an adult must have all of the following for at least 1 month:

- At least one re-experiencing symptom

- At least one avoidance symptom

- At least two arousal and reactivity symptoms

- At least two cognition and mood symptoms

Re-experiencing symptoms
- Flashbacks—reliving the traumatic event, including physical symptoms, such as a racing heart or sweating

- Recurring memories or dreams related to the event

- Distressing thoughts

- Physical signs of stress

Thoughts and feelings can trigger these symptoms, as can words, objects, or situations that are reminders of the event.

Avoidance symptoms
- Staying away from places, events, or objects that are reminders of the experience

- Avoiding thoughts or feelings related to the traumatic event

Avoidance symptoms may cause people to change their routines. For example, some people may avoid driving or riding in a car after a serious car accident.

Arousal and reactivity symptoms

- Being easily startled

- Feeling tense, on guard, or on edge

- Having difficulty concentrating

- Having difficulty falling asleep or staying asleep

- Feeling irritable and having angry or aggressive outbursts

- Engaging in risky, reckless, or destructive behavior

Arousal symptoms are often constant. They can lead to feelings of stress and anger and may interfere with parts of daily life, such as sleeping, eating, or concentrating.

Cognition and mood symptoms

- Trouble remembering key features of the traumatic event

- Negative thoughts about oneself or the world

- Exaggerated feelings of blame directed toward oneself or others

- Ongoing negative emotions, such as fear, anger, guilt, or shame

- Loss of interest in previous activities

- Feelings of social isolation

- Difficulty feeling positive emotions, such as happiness or satisfaction

Cognition and mood symptoms can begin or worsen after the traumatic event. They can lead people to feel detached from friends or family members.

***this is a direct copy from "What is post-traumatic stress disorder, or PTSD?" article found below. In this article you can find more information regarding symptoms for children and teens, and treatments.

U.S. DEPARTMENT OF HEALTH AND HUMAN SERVICES
National Institutes of Health
NIH Publication No. 23-MH-8124
Revised 2023
https://www.nimh.nih.gov/health/publications/post-traumatic-stress-disorder-ptsd#part_11021

PART TWO -From Jo – me

I had 17 of the above 19 symptoms. This was interesting to me to view this article while writing the content of my story and a little shocking as well. I will take you through the symptoms how they were for me with my personal experience.

Re-experiencing symptoms
• Symptoms Flashbacks—reliving the traumatic event, including physical symptoms, such as a racing heart or sweating

For me, I relived the events by thinking daily about them, filled with questions regarding why and what if. This would turn into fearful thoughts that took me to all kinds of places. Daily I experienced fears, doubts and apprehensions about the people in my life and the environment around me. It became terrifying and debilitating.

• Symptoms regarding Distressing thoughts

For me, distressing became terrifying, so much so I feared talking about it, due to the thoughts and the reactions of people in my life. I was also terrified of being committed to mental hospital. I don't know why, but I was terrified. I had never felt so out of control, ever in my entire life, ever, not even close.

• Symptoms Physical signs of stress

For me, I was completely frozen in fear inside of my entire body and my mind, I felt drugged often, I felt like I was seeing myself in a heightened state of panic, not just anxiety, and thinking I was hallucinating while feeling strongly that I was not, and the events happening were very real. To this day, I am not entirely sure what was and what was not really happening. It's getting clearer, though this becomes more and more clear in perspective as I continue to heal.

- Symptoms:Thoughts and feelings can trigger these symptoms, as can words, objects, or situations that are reminders of the event.

Hm yes! This sentence is truer than I can express. Everything triggered me at some point, particularly in the first 3 to 4 months. And then this happened again from situations and individuals around the home my husband I rented, where we intended to find peace and solitude that turned into a horrific retraumatizing extended period. That extended this pain and trauma to be 3 years, and some. The saddest part of the second circumstance, is that it created deep anchors of mistrust that I am still trying to reframe and remove. And this period damaged our lives in every aspect personally, professionally, financially, and more.

Avoidance symptoms
- Staying away from places, events, or objects that are reminders of the experience

Absolutely! I avoided going outside, I tried with my dog as his presence with me was a feeling of protection, however these journeys outside often had circumstances occur that supported all my fears of safety. I simply stopped leaving the house unless I was with both my husband and my dog.

- Avoiding thoughts or feelings related to the traumatic event

This happened in strange ways. At times I it felt like I could watch myself from the outside of my body being either afraid to speak or that it was dangerous for me to speak. Many things happened with people and situations in my life and around me, that made me not sure who or what to trust or feel safe about. Thinking and feeling about these things was a rollercoaster where I would think about it, then panic and hide the thoughts and feelings, shove them back into the corners of my mind. This is truly not helpful, however I can say at the time, or even now viewing it from the outside looking in, rational was not easy.

Arousal and reactivity symptoms

•   Being easily startled

Yes, this intensified by at least 100%.   And if you could go over a 100%, I would say that to. The startle in the moment wouldn't make me scream, it would just make me jump inside and literally freeze. Physically, mentally, emotionally freeze. It felt like being on the outside of my body looking and not feeling, just being stuck. However, the initial split second was panic! Like hitting the button on Jeopardy, the panic stopped in the instant, and then I was left feeling numb.

•   Symptom Feeling tense, on guard, or on edge

All of these and constantly, even certain types of tv shows left me feeling anxiety and anticipation for more anxiety to come. It became hard to find joy in things I found joy in previously.

•   Symptom Having difficulty concentrating

Nothing truer than this one, except the ability to hyper focus on what made me afraid and sometimes analyzing everything in an attempt to understand what the hell happened, for some reason, this I could concentrate on, however not really solve. Otherwise, concentration was lost here and there in everything I did. It made working almost impossible. The numbness would set in with blank thoughts. Something I never experienced. Before PTS I was strong, motivated and I worked like a horse, and I would always walk through fear. Lots of stories about and that was very difficult to observe, that I couldn't find that part of myself.

•   Symptom Having difficulty falling asleep or staying asleep

This thankfully was not to difficult however sometimes dreams would catch a hold of my awareness and keep me thinking about the meaning or message that I might be trying to give myself. I believe if I lost the ability to sleep it would have killed me. Sleep was always something I did well. thankfully

•   Symptom Feeling irritable and having angry or aggressive outbursts

This was a revolving door of angry, outbursts and total frustration, with no sense of control when it came it came like a hailstorm. I think some of this came from being upset with myself going so far off the cliff emotionally and striving to get myself back but not achieving it. The outbursts were very harmful for me, for my husband, for our relationship, and for the animals in our home, they trusted me, and my outburst of yelling sometimes screaming did not make the environment feel safe. I feel deep guilt for this, and this will be difficult to completely overcome.

Cognition and mood symptoms

- Trouble remembering key features of the traumatic event

I don't believe this occurred for me; however, I would have trouble trying to analyze it. I could see all events clearly but did not know how to make sense of it or trust it.

- Symptom of Negative thoughts about oneself or the world

This is hard, I went dark, and I mean darker than ever in my entire life. I had negative thoughts about myself, how could I go so far down emotionally. I had negative thoughts about life and being alive, it didn't feel like it mattered anymore. I had negative thoughts about people in my life that I would never have taken to these thoughts previously. It is like the darkness suffocates you, takes a hold of everything you do, see, hear, feel, and it turns it inside out. It rips you, and who you are to pieces and sits back laughing, watching you try to put yourself back together.

- Symptoms of Exaggerated feelings of blame directed toward oneself or others

I would say that there is a deeper need for those around you to see and help. I am not sure how to put this into words. In the past I could get through anything, and I was not uncomfortable to do it on my own. This situation, the PTSD pulled the rug out from under me, and left me fight less on the floor emotionally and mentally. I needed help desperately and I had no idea how to express this, or how to find it, without being terrified to express it. When my family for example avoided it when I tried to cautiously to talk about it, the feelings of terror were most definitely exaggerated beyond what I normally would ever think or feel. And I was left feeling deeply alone.

- Symptoms of Ongoing negative emotions, such as fear, anger, guilt, or shame

This is true! More than words can possibly express. An endless waterfall of pain, doubt fears guilt, you name it, it flowed through my veins. So polar opposite to who I was before the PTS.

- Symptom of Loss of interest in previous activities

I wouldn't necessarily call it this, to me it felt more like just numb, can't really move numb, can't really think numb. I barely even could smile never mind laugh. Thoughts of joy were in the distant background feeling like a fading memory.

- Symptom of Feelings of social isolation

I felt isolation, I also felt the need to isolate. Neither were helpful. However, when I was social, I found it difficult and very uncomfortable and at the same time I found myself thankful for the time with people also.

- Symptom of Difficulty feeling positive emotions, such as happiness or satisfaction

Yes, difficult to say the least. It simply did not happen for along time. And when it did it was small, short moments then done. Like blowing out the flame on a candle.

I felt detached from everything, everyone, and my own life. This was the most horrible experience of my life and I never wish to go here again. My heart aches profoundly for any person who may be going through this. It is something you just can not comprehend unless you experience it.

What have I learned looking back today? All of these symptoms are just that, symptoms, symptoms of a trauma and it is ok to have experienced them. Experiencing them does not suddenly make me a bad person. It is sad the damage some of them caused, it is sad the changes that have been caused also. Even though I am so much more grounded back to who I was previously. At this point, there is a truth, I have changed. Finding the space to be ok with that will be an evolution, over time.

2 Understanding Hypervigilance After a Traumatic Event

Hyper-vigilance is a state of increased alertness that makes a person excessively watchful of their surroundings. It's often a response to a perceived threat and can be a common aftermath of experiencing traumatic events. This heightened state of anxiety and sensitivity can significantly affect an individual's well-being, making it a topic of considerable concern in the field of mental health.

What is Hyper-vigilance?

Hyper-vigilance involves being on a constant lookout for danger, to the point where it can become overwhelming and exhausting. It's as if the brain is on high alert, trying to protect the individual from potential threats, even when there are none. This can lead to a range of emotional and physical responses, including increased heart rate, rapid breathing, and difficulty focusing on tasks at hand.

The Connection to Trauma

Trauma can profoundly affect the brain's threat detection system. When someone experiences a traumatic event, their brain can become wired to anticipate danger, leading to a state of perpetual alertness. This is often seen in individuals with Post-Traumatic Stress Disorder (PTSD), where hyper-vigilance is a common symptom. The traumatic event can be anything from a natural disaster, serious accident, physical or emotional abuse, to experiences of war or violence.

The Impact on Daily Life

Living in a state of constant alertness can be draining. It may lead to sleep disturbances, as the individual finds it hard to relax and feel safe enough to sleep. Social interactions can also become challenging; individuals may perceive threats in benign social cues or find crowded spaces overwhelming. This can lead to avoidance behaviors, isolation, and can even impact one's ability to work or study.

Managing Hyper-vigilance

While hyper-vigilance can be a challenging symptom to overcome, there are strategies that can help manage its impact:

- **Mindfulness and Relaxation Techniques:** Practices such as guided meditation, deep breathing exercises, and progressive muscle relaxation can help calm the mind and body, reducing feelings of alertness.
- **Cognitive Behavioral Therapy (CBT):** CBT can be effective in helping individuals understand and change thought patterns that contribute to hyper-vigilance.
- **Exposure Therapy:** Gradually exposing individuals to the situations or objects they fear in a controlled way can help reduce sensitivity over time.
- **Physical Activity:** Regular exercise can help reduce anxiety and improve overall well-being.
- **Seeking Professional Help:** A therapist specializing in trauma can offer personalized strategies and support for managing hyper-vigilance.

Hyper-vigilance is a natural response to trauma, but when it starts to interfere with daily life, it becomes imperative to address it. With the right support and strategies, individuals can learn to manage their symptoms, regain a sense of safety, and improve their quality of life. If you or someone you know is struggling with hyper-vigilance, reaching out for professional help can be a significant first step toward recovery.

PART TWO From Jo – me

This was me 100% and the crazy thing is this went in waves of different levels and scenarios due to the circumstances around me.

Initially I was just sensitive, uncomfortable and beginning to watch more carefully than before. I became hyper aware of cars, people, and anything that appeared odd or different. And this got worse, and worse from people around me.

At one point I happened to notice someone who regularly walked their dog and stopping and bending over and looking in the window of my house and that set me off, and I started to have feelings that I was being watched from people in the neighborhood and the person didn't look the same as the person who normally walked the dog, now I don't' actually know for sure today whether that was true or not. I am still fairly comfortable that it was.

When you feel this incredible deep fear of being safe, and not knowing from what exactly, it is debilitating. I mean imagine for a moment someone calls you and tells you there is a threat, that you're in danger but they don't know when and they don't know by who and they don't know why. What do you do? That's how I felt I felt like I was told that, but I wasn't told that. I experienced these experiences that made me feel very much in danger and it was initially like the same thing that just blew up

When you are in this hyper vigilant state everything becomes a threat especially when you don't understand the threat, and simple phrases even become instigators of potential threat real or imaginary. You just don't know, and that is the problem. You just don't know.

I did not know, and to heal I had to move through the terror of being in danger from the unknown, to feeling not in danger and able to protect myself. This took a long time, and it was baby steps here and there.

Today is March 7th, 2024, and I can comfortably say I do not feel that angst of unknown danger or hyper vigilant to the outside anymore. However, now I will always be aware more than before. I don't think that will go away. Laughing out loud here, if someone wants to sneak up on me, even as a joke I don't think it would go well for them. In truth I've changed, I feel strong, but I still feel aware of feeling vulnerable and needing to protect myself from that. And that's where we are today.

3 Navigating Heightened Anxiety: Understanding the Three Aspects of the Human Self

Anxiety, particularly when it reaches heightened levels, can be an overwhelming experience, impacting individuals in multifaceted ways. To navigate through and eventually overcome such periods of intense anxiety, it's essential to understand and address the three core aspects of the human self: the emotional, the mental, and the physical. Each of these play a critical role in both experiencing and managing anxiety, and by acknowledging and working with these aspects, individuals can find more effective ways to cope and heal.

1. The Emotional Aspect: Feeling and Releasing Pain The emotional component of the self is where anxiety is felt most acutely. This aspect encompasses the feelings and emotions that arise during episodes of heightened anxiety, such as fear, worry, or sadness. The key to managing this emotional aspect is in allowing oneself to feel and acknowledge these emotions without judgment. Suppressing or ignoring emotional pain often leads to it manifesting in other ways. Instead, finding safe and healthy outlets for emotional expression, such as talking to a trusted friend or therapist, writing in a journal, or engaging in creative activities, can facilitate the process of release. Recognizing and validating one's emotions is a crucial step in the journey towards managing anxiety.

2. The Mental Aspect: Viewing and Rationalizing Pain The mental aspect involves how we perceive and process our experiences of anxiety. It's the part of us that interprets situations, weighs options, and makes decisions. In the context of heightened anxiety, the mental self can either exacerbate the situation by spiraling into negative thought patterns or contribute to calming the mind by developing rational, constructive solutions. Cognitive techniques, such as mindfulness, cognitive-behavioral strategies, and reframing negative thoughts, are valuable tools for the mental aspect. By

learning to view the situation through a more balanced, rational lens, individuals can reduce the intensity of their anxiety and start to see viable paths forward.

3. The Physical Aspect: Experiencing and Releasing Pressure. Anxiety is not just an emotional and mental experience; it manifests physically as well. The physical aspect refers to how our bodies react to anxiety, often through symptoms like increased heart rate, muscle tension, and rapid breathing. Acknowledging these physical responses is vital. Engaging in activities that help release this physical tension can be immensely beneficial. This might include deep breathing, yoga, regular exercise, or simply taking a moment to relax and rest. The physical self has a powerful influence on the emotional and mental aspects; by calming the body, we can often also calm the mind and emotions.

Heightened anxiety is a complex condition that affects the emotional, mental, and physical dimensions of the human self. Understanding and addressing each of these aspects is crucial in managing and eventually overcoming anxiety. It's about creating a balanced approach that acknowledges and nurtures the whole self - feeling and releasing emotional pain, rationalizing and reframing mental processes, and experiencing and alleviating physical tension. By recognizing and working with these three aspects of our being, individuals can develop more effective strategies for navigating through the challenges of heightened anxiety and move toward a state of greater peace and stability.

PART TWO with Jo - me

Even though the content I've previously written is insightful, practical, and helpful, it's important to acknowledge that applying this knowledge isn't always straightforward. For those who have experienced or are experiencing post-traumatic stress or heightened anxiety, the path to healing can feel particularly challenging. You might find relief in hearing this acknowledged, understanding that it's truly not as simple as it may seem.

I found it difficult to implement any techniques I knew very well as a mind coach. I understand how hard it is.

Over 14 years of working with clients on mindset shifts, reframing thoughts, and implementing strategy changes, I've developed a deep familiarity with these processes. Despite my expertise, there were moments when I struggled to apply these practical strategies into my own life. This difficulty made me question whether the challenge was the process's length or a deeper resistance. Through this journey, I discovered that while I knew the tools theoretically, actively utilizing them required a different approach.

When I became overwhelmed with my thoughts, questions, memories, writing them down was sometimes helpful, sometimes not, intensifying my feelings at times. Yet, this fluctuation seemed to be an essential part of navigating through my emotions.

My experience taught me the importance of comfort and trust in communication, especially with those closest to us. Trust can become a fluctuating force in times of emotional turmoil, as I found out with my husband. I trusted my husband 100% previously. Throughout the PTSD I was like a yo-yo, up and down, trusting him, not trusting him. Deep inside, the memory was there, and then there I was suddenly, constantly trying to remind myself that I believed in him that I trusted him. It was like being disconnected from yourself on and off, over, and over. Like power surges. Despite my deep trust in my husband, and my trust in others my emotional state led me to doubt this trust, illustrating the internal conflict many of us face during such times.

I see even more how the work that I was doing prior to my episode was beneficial and helpful with clients. Because my practice was actively listening, so that I could really understand what my clients were feeling, what they were experiencing and what the block was, what was getting in the way. In this kind of heightened anxiety, you don't know what's getting in your way. You just know the story. And the repercussion of the story is a mind trapped in a cage trying to find a key or a mechanism to get out of the cage.

I've come to understand that healing is a complex journey requiring patience and small, manageable steps rather than attempting to address everything simultaneously. Finding activities or practices that provide comfort, and someone who listens without judgment or interference, is crucial. This process of releasing emotions, whether through conversation or writing, is an integral part of healing.

I would say there is no right or wrong way to find something physical to help the body through. As each of us has our own likes in this area. However, I do believe finding a meditation audio will definitely help. The principle of going into meditative states of quieting the mind, and the principles of hypnosis, of distracting the mind to go into meditative states, essentially provide an easy way to allow the body to breath deeply and regularly. This is essential. I know, I was holding my breath constantly in the that feeling of angst, and I knew better. One audio helped me and there was only the one that I listened to, because to much change was simply to much for me.

4 Wolve's in Sheep's Clothing: Advocacy and Betrayal a Reflection on Personal Struggles with PTS

In the world of mental health advocacy, the expectation is often that those who speak up for the vulnerable, especially for women struggling with anxiety and Post-Traumatic Stress (PTS), embody the principles of empathy, understanding, and support. However, it is a devastating realization when someone who presents themselves as a champion for these causes becomes the very source of harm they profess to stand against. Here we delve into the intricate and painful situation where a supposed advocate uses an individual's personal suffering and experiences with PTS not as a means to aid, but as a tool for insult and self-victimization.

The Ideal Advocate: Ideally, an advocate for women and those dealing with anxiety and PTS is someone who listens, empathizes, and uses their position to amplify the voices of the suffering. They should be a safe harbor, offering solace and understanding, and aiding in the healing process. Their role is to be a bridge between the pain of personal experience and the hope of recovery and support.

The Betrayal: The betrayal occurs when this expectation is shattered - when the individual who is supposed to be a pillar of support turns into a perpetrator of pain. This betrayal is particularly insidious because it comes cloaked in the guise of advocacy. When a person who has spoken publicly about being a proponent for those with PTS turns their back on these very principles, it is a stark reminder of the complexities and contradictions that can exist within human behavior.

The Impact of Betrayal: For someone struggling with PTS, this kind of betrayal can be retraumatizing. It is not just a breach of trust; it is an assault on their journey towards healing. When their own experiences with PTS are used against them, especially by someone they believed to be an ally, it can exacerbate feelings of vulnerability, isolation, and distrust. This can have a profound impact on their mental health and overall well-being.

Understanding the Perpetrator: Understanding the mindset and motivations of someone who betrays trust in such a manner is complex. It raises questions about the authenticity of their advocacy. Are their public declarations a mask for deeper, unresolved issues? Is their advocacy conditional, only offered when it serves their interests? These questions point to the unsettling possibility that their commitment to the cause may be superficial or self-serving.

Healing and Moving Forward: For those who have experienced this betrayal, the path to healing involves recognizing that the actions of one individual do not define the entire journey of recovery. It's essential to seek support from genuine, empathetic individuals and professionals who understand the nuances of PTS. The importance of finding a compassionate and authentic support system cannot be overstated.

The journey of healing from PTS is full of challenges, and the added pain of betrayal by someone who was trusted can make it even more difficult. However, it is important to remember that this betrayal is a reflection of the perpetrator's failings, not the victims. Healing is possible, and with the right support, individuals can emerge stronger, more resilient, and more empowered in their journey towards recovery.

PART TWO with Jo - me

My experience with this was brutal! It was more harmful and intensified my heightened anxiety to the extreme place of barely being able to bare the emotional tornado's exploding inside every part of me mentally, emotionally, and physically.

I wrote this chapter to address a concerning reality: the existence of individuals who exploit those in need under the guise of being advocates or practitioners of potentially harmful healing modalities. That also present themselves as caring sensitive people. This is very dangerous for those in the state of PTS, and I met one during the time I was starting to heal, that retraumatized me with intention. This person presents as a female advocate with a modality for helping those with PTSD and anxiety. A modality I do not advocate and would never use or suggest used under "heightened anxiety", because heightened anxiety is a state of hyper suggestibility and requires careful healing tools that do not add to this state.

However, I thought perhaps this person was decent and caring from their representation of supporting females and people in PTS or anxiety. I WAS VERY WRONG!

Not only was this false advocate a female, who very calculatingly presented kindness to gain a relationship, she was a landlord to a home my family rented, in particular to seek quiet, peace and solace so healing could occur.

Many issues and circumstance occurred at this property. I reached a point of distress feeling it necessary to express personal details of my situation and our family trying to heal, and that circumstances at this property, our home, was inflicting further harm. The response was shocking. I still to this day can not fathom the blatant indifference ingrained in this person's nature or character, claiming to be an advocate for women and healing. There came no actions of concern or emotional investment, other than to use my PTS to cause further harm.

These actions robbed me of two and half years of potential healing. And most certainly retraumatized me. This whole situation then caused my husband to be traumatized. Something I had difficulty seeing until after we moved, and some form of healing breath could move through me. I am still in a spin of thoughts and feelings of how our relationship survived. And hoping it actually did without wounds so deep they simply can not heal.

I will not easily come to a place of finding forgiveness in this story or the persons involved at that time. Perhaps forgiving myself for not being able to see or feel the instinctual part of me, that may have helped me make choices and decisions during this time to get away from there rather than fight to heal. I was desperate for peace, and I did not find it until leaving this location. The damage was devasting.

It was all I could do but fight to heal. Because healing meant I would survive. And wanting to survive was a seesaw of emotions and belief. Today this still causes me to feel deep pain in the knowing I felt dark thoughts of wanting to just die. I have never come close to this before, and it is a new thing to rectify within myself. It challenges my strength, by belief in my strength, and that is painful and frustrating at the same time.

So, what do I do? I try to accept the experience as an experience. And in having the experience I gain more awareness in many ways that hopefully will continue to help me help others. With that I can remember who I am, how strong I am, and that I have always appeared to have a purpose of helping others so this situation can only help me to do that moving forward. And moving forward is the key.

I graciously end this chapter by saying "this wolf in sheep's clothing" can kiss my ass!!! I am so much stronger than you can imagine. And I am grateful to know I am a better person even after you and your ignorance!

To any of you who may be suffering or suffered from others. YOU ARE GOOD ENOUGH! You can be ok! They are not ok. Hold on, find something to motivate you to move forward! Be a crow look for the shining things that are good to you.

5 The Impact of Authority figures Misunderstanding in Individuals with Post-Traumatic Stress

For individuals grappling with Post-Traumatic Stress (PTS), interactions with authority figures can be pivotal moments in their journey towards healing or can unfortunately lead to further trauma. When these authority figures – be they law enforcement, medical professionals, or others in positions of power – misread or misunderstand a situation involving someone with PTS, the consequences can be deeply damaging. This article delves into the implications of such misunderstandings and emphasizes the need for a careful, empathetic approach in dealing with individuals experiencing PTS.

The Significance of Understanding in Authority:

Individuals in positions of authority often have the power to significantly alter the course of a person's life, especially in critical situations. For someone with PTS, a supportive and understanding response from an authority figure can be a lifeline, offering a sense of safety and validation. Conversely, a response that stems from misinterpretation or a lack of empathy can exacerbate the individual's fear and distrust, potentially deepening their trauma.

Consequences of Misunderstanding PTS:

When an individual with PTS is misunderstood or their condition is misinterpreted by those in authority, several damaging outcomes can occur:

1. **Increased Fear and Distrust**: A negative experience can reinforce the person's fear that they are not safe or that their concerns are not valid, leading to increased feelings of vulnerability and isolation.

2. **Worsening of Symptoms**: Such encounters can trigger or worsen PTS symptoms, including anxiety, flashbacks, and sleep disturbances.

3. **Reluctance to Seek Help**: Negative experiences can lead to a reluctance to reach out for help in the future, out of fear of being misunderstood or mistreated again.

The Importance of Effective Communication is crucial when dealing with individuals suffering from PTS. Authority figures must be trained to ask the right questions and to listen actively and empathically. It's not enough to simply gather information; understanding the individual's mental and emotional state is vital. This approach helps in creating a complete and accurate picture of the situation, preventing snap judgments or decisions based on incomplete understanding.

Training and Awareness for Authority Figures:

To mitigate the risks of misunderstanding and misinterpretation, training and increased awareness for those in positions of authority are essential. This training should focus not just on the symptoms and dynamics of PTS but also on effective communication strategies and the importance of empathy and patience in interactions with individuals affected by PTS.

The role of authority figures in the lives of individuals with PTS cannot be understated. Misunderstandings in these interactions can have deeply harmful effects, leaving the individual in a heightened state of fear and potentially worsening their condition. It is imperative that those in authority positions are equipped with the knowledge and skills to understand and effectively assist individuals with PTS. Only through thoughtful, informed, and empathetic engagement can the needs of those with PTS be adequately met, fostering an environment of trust and support crucial for their healing journey.

PART TWO with Jo -me

This chapter is particularly difficult for me, which is why I felt compelled to write it. Various circumstances, such as abuse or stalking, can lead to Post-Traumatic Stress or heightened anxiety. The response individuals receive from authorities in such situations is crucial to their sense of safety.

Years ago, I experienced stalking from a man who initially called my home for a sales pitch. He fell in love with my voice from my answering machine message and began calling multiple times a day. The calls escalated, with him calling in the middle of the night. He never spoke until one day he left a message about the sunrise. I panicked, I felt as though he was watching the sunrise outside my house. In fear, I went to the local police. They handled my situation with genuine care, took me seriously, and found the man within six hours. They informed him that if he contacted me again, he would be arrested. This support made me feel safe and the situation was resolved.

In contrast, when we rented a home intended to bring peace during this troublesome time of my episodes of PTSD, our landlord falsely involved the police, creating a very distressing experience. While the initial officer handled the situation rather well, another interaction with law enforcement left me feeling abandoned and misunderstood. Our landlords retaliated by turning off our internet, and when we called the police for help, their response was unsupportive and aggressive. Due to poor cell service, we relied on Wi-Fi calling, leading to a frustrating back-and-forth with the authorities. One female officer in particular, was curt and dismissive, failing to understand our situation despite our file clearly stating we were being harassed. She advised me to confront our landlords, which was not only impactful but also dangerous.

This further retraumatized me, as our landlords continued their harassment without consequences. The law, as it stood, left us feeling unprotected. We hired a lawyer, incurring significant financial losses. Our landlords tried to force us to remove security measures like cameras, motion lights, and the window coverings in the home we lived in, making us feel incredibly vulnerable. We were desperate to leave but couldn't do so quickly without facing homelessness.

This experience shattered my faith in the legal system. I understand that law enforcement officers have a very difficult job and often develop a "thick skin." However, during this time, I felt profoundly unprotected and misunderstood. The lack of thorough investigation and empathy from the authorities had devastating consequences for us, leaving us feeling unsafe and financially drained. This chapter underscores the critical need for proper handling and support in such traumatic situations.

The saddest part of these events is that they are solely separate to the original events that ignited heightened anxiety for me and that they are directly responsible for keeping me in this state for far longer than necessary.

6 The Critical Role of Hope in Healing from Post-Traumatic Stress

In the challenging journey of healing from Post-Traumatic Stress (PTS), hope stands out as a beacon of resilience and recovery. While coping mechanisms and therapeutic interventions are crucial, the role of hope cannot be overstated. Hope is a fundamental force that propels individuals through the tumultuous waters, especially when grappling with heightened anxiety. Here we will cover the power of hope in healing from PTSD and why it is often considered a lifesaver for those struggling with this condition.

The Essence of Hope in Healing:

Hope is the driving force that encourages individuals to look beyond their current struggles and believe in the possibility of a better future. In the context of PTS, hope plays a multifaceted role. It helps individuals imagine a life beyond their trauma, providing a sense of purpose and direction. Hope instills the belief that healing is possible, change is possible, even when the journey seems overwhelming.

Counteracting the Grip of Anxiety:

For those stuck in the cycle of heightened anxiety that often accompanies PTS, hope offers a way out. It acts as a counterbalance to the fear and despair that can dominate their thoughts. Hope introduces a positive narrative in the midst of negative thought patterns, offering a glimpse of light in what might seem like unending darkness. This shift in perspective is crucial, as it can reduce the intensity of anxiety and open the door to more effective coping strategies.

Hope as a Catalyst for Action:

Beyond providing comfort, hope motivates action. It inspires individuals to engage in their recovery actively, whether by seeking professional help, embracing therapeutic practices, or making lifestyle changes that support their well-being. Hope energizes and empowers, transforming massive suffering into proactive healing.

The Science Behind Hope and Healing: Research in psychology and neuroscience supports the significance of hope in the healing process. A hopeful outlook has been linked to better stress management, improved mental health, and even physical health benefits. For individuals with PTS, hope can enhance the effectiveness of therapy, increase resilience, and improve overall quality of life.

Nurturing Hope in the Midst of PTS:

Cultivating hope in the face of PTS requires conscious effort. It can be nurtured through various means, such as connecting with supportive communities, engaging in meaningful activities, and practicing mindfulness and positive thinking. Personal narratives and testimonies of those who have navigated similar paths can also be powerful sources of hope.

In the journey of recovery from Post-Traumatic Stress, hope is not just a nice-to-have; it is an essential, life-saving element. It provides the strength to endure, the courage to face fears, and the vision to see beyond the pain. For anyone struggling with the heightened anxiety of PTS, fostering a sense of hope can be a pivotal step towards healing and reclaiming a life marked by resilience and growth. Remember, in the darkest moments of PTS, the flicker of hope can illuminate the path to a brighter tomorrow.

Hope comes from feeling there is light at the end of the tunnel. From feeling understood, heard, and experiencing a genuine concern or comfort from people.

Hope thrives on feeling acknowledged, heard, and genuinely cared for. It's about believing there's a brighter future ahead. Hope is not just a nice-to-have; it's fundamental to our well-being.

Hope is vital! It is given to others through understanding, empathy and compassion.

PART TWO with Jo -me

Wow this is a tough one. In my years as a mind coach, I've seen firsthand the significant role hope plays in my clients' journeys toward healing and growth. A crucial quality of an effective coach, mentor, or counselor is their natural ability to help clients reconnect with hope.

During my struggles with heightened anxiety, I lost the ability to see hope or feel it, and most definitely lost a connection to it, particularly during the period of being re-traumatized. That period was more traumatic than I could bare. Hope was gone and no one in my life was able to see I needed that or managed to give me hope even by accident.

Looking back, I believe so many people were/are very affected by the experience of COVID 19. That alone was a global event that caused levels of anxiety, trauma PTSD etc. that will take years to analyze. How could the people in my life possibly be able to help me with my intense situation while they were struggling through their own levels known or unknown.

Hope would have been extremely helpful for me. When you watch the world around you act in a manner that is not caring or kind, and you're in desperation to be understood and in need of help, kindness understanding and compassion it takes all the hope from you. And this kills the soul slowly.

Specific things shocked me during my struggle, and they crushed hope for me. It was so far gone from my belief or awareness I did not even realize it. I am not sure when the tiny spark ignited again. I believe it was lit and blown out periodically while we worked with our lawyer. Thankful for him! However, he battled legal tape and deception from our landlords also, hence the see saw, but hope was swinging in and out. I think it came in a deep breath of relief when we finally were able to move. Perhaps a month later, after the shear exhaustion began to subside. And then it simply grew. Thank God!

I am here to tell you today, there is light at the end of the tunnel, don't let the mind let go of hope, even if it can't be felt. Hope is alive, and it needs time to grow.

7 Navigating Communication Challenges in Heightened Anxiety of PTS: The Need for Patience and Awareness

One of the less discussed but significant impacts of Post-Traumatic Stress (PTS) is its effect on communication. Heightened anxiety associated with PTS can lead to a disconnection between one's thoughts and speech, where the mind and mouth seem to operate out of sync. This phenomenon often results in the expression of thoughts and feelings that were not intended, creating misunderstandings and frustration both for the individual with PTS and their listeners.

The Disconnect Between Mind and Mouth:

During episodes of heightened anxiety associated with PTS, the brain's normal processing speed can be disrupted. This disruption can lead to a lag or disconnect between what the individual intends to say and what is actually articulated. The result is often speech that may seem disjointed, overly emotional, or even contradictory. This disconnect is not a reflection of the individual's cognitive abilities but rather a symptom of the heightened state of anxiety.

Misinterpretations and Misunderstandings:

Given this disconnect, what is said by someone experiencing PTS may be misinterpreted by others, leading to misunderstandings. It's important for both parties – the individual with PTS and the listener – to recognize that these moments do not accurately reflect the person's true intentions or thoughts. Awareness of this potential misalignment is crucial in avoiding unnecessary conflicts or hurt feelings.

The Role of Patience in Communication:

Patience becomes an invaluable tool in such scenarios. For those interacting with someone experiencing heightened anxiety from PTS, it's important to practice patience, giving the individual time to fully articulate their thoughts. Rushing or pressuring them to speak more quickly can exacerbate their anxiety and further impair communication.

Strategies for Effective Communication:

For individuals with PTS, certain strategies can aid in bridging the communication gap. Techniques such as pausing before responding, writing down thoughts before speaking, or even using non-verbal communication can be helpful. It's also beneficial for them to inform their conversation partners about their challenges with communication, fostering understanding and patience.

Creating an Environment of Understanding:

Both parties can work towards creating an environment where communication is approached with understanding and compassion. This involves actively listening, avoiding assumptions, and asking clarifying questions, when needed. It also means being open to discussing and addressing any communication barriers that arise.

The challenges in communication stemming from the heightened anxiety of PTS require both awareness and patience from all who are involved. Understanding the disconnect that can occur between the mind and mouth during these times is key to fostering effective communication. By approaching conversations with empathy, patience, and a willingness to adapt, individuals with PTS can feel more understood and supported, aiding in their overall journey of healing and recovery.

PART TWO with Jo -me

Wow, this one is tough to circle back, view and speak to. Remembering the many disconnected moments thoughts, words, the miscommunication and the lack of patience in communication. Where to start? And how to start without being too emotional?

Let me say this with certainty, there is a vey significant disconnect between word and mouth for a period of time. Most definitely when encompassed in the heightened anxiety. It is like a kink in a watering hose or shall I say a few kinks. You have to stop and unkink to let the flow get through. But sometimes words come out that aren't quite what was intended, and this also puts a kink in the flow.

There were many times I found myself stopping and staring, and as I've said blank. Sometimes it was to wait for what words were intended and sometimes it was because they just were not there to be found. This was very frustrating for me. I felt weak, I felt broken, and I was scared constantly of saying the wrong thing. The polar opposite of what I have ever been regarding communication. I still at times find it difficult to respond, or I'm not sure what it is, maybe I am just a little bit different.

Patience turned into frustration and sometimes panic itself. In other words, I had no patience, not only from trying to find patients in communicating, but from trying to have patience with others. It is like the anxiety reaches up and chokes you, you panic, and you literally do not know what to do. Honestly figuring out what to say when it was necessary for me to say something was simply an outburst of thoughts and feelings with no control. Like a pipe bursting and there you are stuck with gushing water.

Actively listening, avoiding assumptions, and asking clarifying questions was important for me to try and navigate just as much as it was very important for those around to me to do also.

I feel a lot of time was added onto my "prison sentence" of PTS due to those 3 factors missing from more than a few people, including myself. However, I no longer feel guilty for my communication flubs. I needed help, I needed patience and I most certainly needed understanding and compassionate responses regardless.

It is sad to write this, and truly realize the damage caused to me when I was desperate trying to give awareness of my PTS to some who gave little to no compassionate response.

As I said it lengthened the "prison of emotional trauma" I was in, and the depths of anxiety and loss drive for life I fell deeper into.

I wrote the details of the beginning of this chapter from the mind coach perspective looking at the circumstances, as it is very true. However, from personal experience as a PTS victim, it is extremely difficult to pause and formulate thoughts perspectives etc. Writing helps this a lot, but even writing can be all over in clarity, however it helps to put the anchors there, that will eventually guide back to a better mental space. Communication is the most difficult thing at all levels under the binding chains of heightened anxiety.

Communication has mixed signals and misinterpretations in so many ways under everyday normal circumstances it does not need the added influence, barriers and misunderstandings of PTSD or heightened anxiety at any level. Patience and compassion is the only process to follow.

8 The Art of Listening: A Key Approach in Helping Individuals with Heightened Anxiety

In the realm of mental health, particularly in addressing PTS and heightened anxiety, the power of effective listening often goes unrecognized. Active listening, characterized by empathy and understanding, is not just a communication skill but a therapeutic tool that can be given by anyone, not just a professional. It involves listening, not with the intent to respond, but with the goal to truly understand and provide comfort. The art of listening can be a crucial element in offering support to those experiencing anxiety, enabling them to feel heard, understood, and safe.

The Importance of Active Listening: For individuals grappling with anxiety, being able to express their thoughts and feelings without fear of judgment or interruption is invaluable. Active listening provides this space. It involves paying full attention, acknowledging the person's feelings, and reflecting back what is heard without immediately offering advice or solutions. This approach shows the individual that their feelings are valid and they are not alone in their experience.

Creating a Safe Space Through Listening: Listening to understand lays the foundation for a safe and supportive environment. It allows individuals with anxiety to explore their thoughts and emotions without the pressure of being fixed or judged. This validation is often the first step in helping them navigate through their anxiety. When a person feels truly heard, it can reduce the intensity of their anxious feelings, providing a sense of relief and calm.

The Role of Empathy in Listening: Empathy is at the heart of effective listening. It involves putting oneself in the other person's shoes and understanding their perspective. For someone with anxiety, interacting with someone who empathizes with their situation can be incredibly comforting. Empathy doesn't mean having all the answers; it's about showing genuine concern and understanding.

Responding After Listening: Once the individual has been fully heard, responses should be thoughtful and considerate, aimed at providing comfort rather than quick fixes. The listener can offer reassurance, validate the person's feelings, and gently guide them towards helpful perspectives or resources. The key is to ensure that the individual feels supported and not overwhelmed.

The Limitations of Listening: While listening is a powerful tool, it's important to acknowledge its limitations. In cases of severe anxiety, professional help may be required. Listening can be the first step in encouraging individuals to seek further support from therapists or counselors who specialize in anxiety disorders.

The act of listening, when done with empathy and without judgment, can be a profound way to assist those dealing with anxiety. It creates a bridge of understanding and trust, essential for providing effective support. By prioritizing active listening, we can offer a safe haven for individuals to express themselves and begin their journey towards managing their anxiety. Remember, sometimes the most impactful thing we can do for someone is to simply, listen.

PART TWO with Jo -me

I realize even more now, how much people don't really listen. I kind of new this before. I mean stop thinking, and listen, stop thinking about what to say, how to respond or how to defend but actually stop, focus and listen. This implies to when a person speaks and to when a person writes. I say this this way trying to be clear.

This is how communication issues develop; they begin and sometimes grow in the "not listening" and equally in the "not being heard".

I always knew this to some level, probably more subconsciously than always consciously in the past. It is likely why, throughout my life people found me to talk to, and why I was successful when becoming a mind coach/hypnotherapist, I prefer thought coach. Also, why my husband likes to call me "Jesus" as he has, for years watched strangers begin to tell their stories to me and found it endearing to watch me listen to each one without judgment only empathy and compassion.

My time struggling in heightened emotions of traumatic stress froze me in many ways. It stole this part of me for a longer period of time than I am comfortable with. Thankfully I have been recovering this ability. It also stole my ability to easily express what was occurring with me, even to myself. Sometimes I wonder if this wasn't actually the case at all, and that it was others around me just could not comprehend. In these moments, I always felt alone, a feeling so deep and filled with grief that I never in my life have felt before. Even now as I articulate this, I can feel that feeling just from the memory.

It is a strong bolder of emotion planted into my subconscious. It is heavy, it is black like the night sky without stars, and it will take time to chip it away

It is uncomfortable to express this as it leaves me with feelings of not being strong, and that is just not true, but the moment that it is felt, is impacting, as it pushes me, like it is trying to make me fall again. I have to stop and remind myself how strong I am, how strong I was before, and that strength is not gone it's just being pushed back from the memories of feeling such deep devasting fears.

I try now to look at this as if it was bully poking at me, this makes me giggle inside sometimes as I would never allow someone to do that to me physically and this helps me push back emotionally to give space for my strength to rise stronger and stronger.

I am sure there are people around me that just want me to be the old me, I understand as they need the old me. This is difficult sometimes because for the fist time in my life I needed, more than any of them can even imagine. And even today, I sometimes feel moments that I want to just scream from the vibration of that anxiety still stuck inside. It penetrated every cell in my body. Imagine blowing up a balloon, you know the ones that are difficult and just won't get started, by the time it finally starts filling you are out of breath already. You blow and blow filling that balloon determined to get it done, all the while running out of air, and you feel that pressure building "breathe" "take a breath" you don't until finally you can't take it anymore and you let go breathe and all the air squeezes out of the ballon. There is a crazy sense of relief felt.

Now imagine not being able to let go of the balloon and take that breath, the body expanding inside itself in full panic to breathe. All you can manage is inhale a small bit to survive while still holding tightly. Not only is the emotional mental fear happening but a physical fear within the cells screaming inside the body for oxygen. This is what I felt like for many, many months, and many times through the 3 years.

I can say this confidently, the "think positive", "change the perspective" coaching is not that simple under the influence of heightened anxiety and PTS. I understand how exasperatingly difficult it is. There are no words that can easily explain this. Even when you try to think positive or change the thoughts, each time is a different experience however most simply don't get through.

Looking back, it often felt just like I would go blank, and literally experience feeling no thought, just seeing things in front of me but not even labeling them. Like staring blankly out the window at the trees but not even thinking "trees", just nothing.

From my years of mental coaching this would be viewed as "resistance" it is not a conscious resistance it is subconscious from the trauma stress filling ever corner of your being. The only way through this is to allow the time to slowly let it go.

I don't really like to call it 'energy" in this perspective it is a form of existence all on its own, negative energy is one thing, but traumatic stress is something entirely different and it is, soul sucking. It strives to have a life of its own.

I needed to talk it out and be listened to, most importantly heard, no one was able to do this that was close to me, and I struggled in even thinking about finding someone professionally. Mostly because, here I was a mind coach that fell right the hell of the cliff emotionally. My husband tried, and it was very hard, hard on him emotionally, he simply did not know what to do. He also was frozen in the level of emotional outbursts that came from me, something I simply did not do with him previously, we barely ever argued, but we argued more in these 3 years than our entire 18 years together. I saw the deep sadness as he watched me, and I saw him with fierce strength hold back his own tears seeing me in so much pain. Having no idea what to do.

Some of my family new something happened that scared the hell out of me, but they did not realize how bad that shock and fear grew. However, no one took the time to actively ask and listen to me. There were moments I felt very hurt by my family appearing to skirt around the subject not understanding or seeing how bad it was for me. I knew they were always in a belief that I was strong and was ok. This was a new experience for them also. I was usually the one everyone could count on to be strong and not feel these kinds of feelings. I realize now that they too may have been navigating their own life struggles trying not to burden me.

The only way for me to explain this pain is to say "imagine drowning in a lake splashing, choking, and sinking, the people closest to you are on the shore watching, they know you can swim, they don't think there is anything really wrong, so they do nothing, you are left there, and you are drowning. And you are TERRIFIED!

I know they did not intend to hurt me or harm me, this simply is not who they are as people. "The old Jo holds on to this" "the new one still has moments that burn into the heart being pierced with a hot arrow". This too will take time to let go.

The damage emotionally is done, the trust is cracked, this one is hard to navigate through.

I feel trust is extremely important to be able to rely on when trapped in heightened anxiety. These emotions and fear become a new foundation within you. Trust to me was more important than ever before. Feeling that I can trust those around me was essential and sadly more often, I did not feel this way. I was terrified who I could trust sometimes, and this is very hard to explain.

I stood in many showers and simply cried. When it was really bad, I sat on the shower floor and bawled my eyes out, desperate for? I don't even know, just to cry and cry like never before. The pain was totally encompassing, the fight in me was totally gone in those moments.

Sometimes these were dangerous moments, as this is where the darkness can put out the light to live.

I will be forever sad that I ever experienced thoughts of dying, in the past I had no comprehension of what that could possibly feel like. However, on a different note I am now very aware of what that feels like and I know if encountering someone in this place, I can truly find a deeper compassion than ever before.

So, I say, Just Don't Let Go, the light of life comes back around, it finds its way through the cracks and the seams of the dark heavy coat being worn emotionally. I say this because I've lived it, I've breathed it and I'm here today trying to help anyone else understand you can get through.

Just Don't Let Go!

9 Navigating the Devastating Losses Associated with Post-Traumatic Stress

Post-Traumatic Stress (PTS) is not just a condition marked by psychological and emotional challenges; it also brings with it a cascade of losses that can profoundly impact every facet of one's life. Individuals grappling with PTS often face significant changes or losses in relationships, employment, personal well-being, and their overall sense of self. This article delves into the various dimensions of loss associated with PTS, shedding light on how these changes can sometimes feel irreparable and the impact they have on the lives of those affected.

1.   **Relationships and Social Connections:** One of the most profound impacts of PTS is on relationships. The strain of coping with the symptoms of PTS can lead to misunderstandings, emotional distance, and sometimes, the breakdown of significant relationships. Marriages may become strained or end, friendships can grow distant, and family dynamics may alter. The individual with PTS might withdraw socially, driven by feelings of fear, shame, or a desire not to burden others, leading to a sense of isolation and loneliness.

2.   **Employment and Financial Stability:** The effects of PTS can extend into professional life, affecting performance, reliability, and the ability to maintain employment. Challenges such as difficulty concentrating, heightened anxiety, and irregular sleep patterns can make regular work difficult. This can lead to job loss, reduced income, and in severe cases, long-term unemployment. The financial strain exacerbates the stress and can feed into a cycle of anxiety and depression.

3.   **Loss of Time and Life Experiences:** Individuals with PTS often find that significant amounts of time are consumed by their condition. Time that might have been spent on hobbies, interests, or personal growth is instead taken up by therapy, coping strategies, and dealing with the symptoms of PTS. This loss of time can feel like missing out on life's experiences, leading to feelings of regret and frustration.

4.   **Joy, Happiness, and Mental Well-Being:** PTS can cast a long shadow over one's ability to experience joy and happiness. The persistent nature of traumatic memories and anxiety can diminish life's pleasures and make it difficult to engage in activities that once brought happiness. This loss of enjoyment can lead to a profound sense of grief for the life one had before the onset of PTS.

5.   **Self-Esteem and Self-Confidence:** The challenge of living with PTS can take a toll on an individual's self-esteem and self-confidence. The ongoing struggle with symptoms, coupled with the losses in other areas of life, can lead to feelings of inadequacy, failure, and a diminished sense of self-worth. This erosion of self-esteem makes it even more challenging to cope with the condition and move forward.

The losses associated with Post-Traumatic Stress are multidimensional and deeply impactful. They extend beyond the individual to touch every aspect of their life. While these changes can sometimes feel irreparable, it's important to recognize that healing and recovery are possible. With the right support, therapy, and coping strategies, individuals can work through their trauma, rebuild their lives, and regain a sense of control and hope. This journey of healing from PTS is not just about managing symptoms but also about reclaiming the aspects of life that have been lost to the condition.

Part Two with Jo – me

This chapter is truly important to be aware of and hopefully give comprehension from a personal perspective. The caliber of damage that can rip through a person's life due to PTSD from trauma is like an explosion that will hit other targets as well.

1.   **Relationships and Social Connections:** the description I wrote for this was more than true in all ways for me. Looking back, I can see how marriages crumble and relationships end or change drastically. All are equally devasting as the PTSD itself. I may not have survived if my husband was not strong enough to endure what we went through together inside our relationship or from the outside that attacked liked wasps that just

won't quit. The relationship for me towards others in my life became strained and uncomfortable to handle from the fear of any judgment or confrontation, that I became less open to socialize even with my own family. And that itself was extremely painful for me to handle or acknowledge to be able to overcome.

2. **Employment and Financial Stability:** 100% true and extremely difficult to avoid. The reason I say this, is there is no room within the struggle of PTSD emotionally to foresee its extensions into this part of ones life. Our life was destroyed professionally and financially. Financially we lost more savings that we could survive the loss from at our stage in life. This in most part was because of the second events that re-traumatized me, that then caused trauma to my husband as well.

The loss financially from legal fees fighting of perpetrators and a system that is massively broken, itself was devastating. Then there was more loss from the exorbitant cost of moving to and from a distant location, then moving twice afterwards as we had to find temporary housing to get away. While still fighting off our landlords.

COVID-19 devasted my coaching practice, which at the time surprised me, however I see how most people during that time did not need as much help, or could not afford it, until near the end and afterwards. Then, moving into the second trauma made me very uncomfortable to even think about working with clients. Two reasons. First, I did not feel it ethical for me to put on a face of strength when I was not, and second, the environment we were in simply was very unstable, invasive, and privacy wise due to our landlords' actions, as I state in this book I am starting over.

The devastation squeezed it's way into my husbands employment at the time also, were he financially lost in magnitude, due to lack of inquiry and compassion from those in charge around him, (this is another story and his private story so that is all I will say) Other than people expect people to suck it up, be strong, move on, get over it, often. They do this without attempting to understand fully a person's situation. My husband did not miss one day of work, and he endured attack and insult from me at home and some inside his work environment while he continued to do his job and make the company money. Kindness and compassion go a long way, he was not given this courtesy, and for this I will forever feel guilty to be part of that cause and effect.

3. **Loss of Time and Life Experiences:** This was massive, we lost 3 plus years of time and joyful experience, or ability to create fond memories. There were moments, but they were destroyed, in particular from the compounding effects of the second events. Particularly as we were in a beautiful location that was 200+ steps to the ocean and hiking trails everywhere around us. We purchased paddleboards, kayaks and gear for ourselves and family if they were to visit. None of them were ever used, as we essentially became hostages to the trauma outside of home, feeling the need to stay inside of our home to protect ourselves, our belongings, and our animals from further harm. We lost valuable time with family having to cancel a planned family summer visit due to the environment. That in the end, was even more harmful than we could have ever imagined, as we had not been together for over 6 years, in part also from COVID-19, and once out of the situation, a devastating illness occurred that is needless to say to loss caused.

The world opened back up late 2021 after COVIDs lockdown. Sadly, it did not open up for us officially until 2024.

4. **Joy, Happiness, and Mental Well-Being:** I have to say little here as the loss of this is expressed so much throughout this book. However, I will say even though I now finally feel a sense of well-being, I still find moments that I feel disconnected to joy or happiness. I don't know why, or what it is. I also do not know how to explain it. I see these moments and they hurt me, a lot, because it is a piece of myself lost or broken that I don't know how to fix.

5. **Self-Esteem and Self-Confidence:** Truer than anything! For me this is a yo-yo effect. In and out, up and down, never in complete control. More so in recent times, as I finish writing now being June 30, 2024, I definitely and thankfully am feeling more connected to my old sense of esteem and confidence. The one niggling thing that gets in this way now is the fact that I and we, my husband and I are starting over in so many ways professionally, financially and rebuilding our relationship back to what it used to be. All

while being terrified inside of how much time we have left to achieve this, neither of us is young. He is in his 60's and I am almost there also.

We were strong enough to make it through what we did. I pray every day that we make it.

Little by little we let go of pain, and loss.

Healing is a journey with a pace of its own.

Open the doors and windows within your heart and

Let the light, and fresh air in!

~Jo Harris

10 The overlap of PTSD and the Seen Stages of Grief

The journey of healing from Post-Traumatic Stress (PTS) and heightened anxiety often mirrors the well-known seven stages of grief, with unique nuances. Those suffering from PTS and anxiety endure not only the typical stages of grief but also grapple with profound undercurrents of fear and loss of self-confidence. These additional layers add complexity to each stage, influencing the order and the outcome of the healing process.

1. **Shock and Denial**: The initial response to trauma or anxiety often involves shock – a numbing disbelief that creates a temporary buffer against the reality of the situation. However, in the context of PTS and anxiety, this shock is frequently compounded by intense fear and a denial that extends beyond the event itself to a denial of one's emotional turmoil and vulnerability.

2. **Pain and Guilt**: As the shock wears off, it is replaced by suffering and guilt. This stage is particularly intensified in PTS and heightened anxiety, as individuals may blame themselves for their condition or for events beyond their control. This self-blame erodes confidence and can make the pain feel more acute and personal.

3. **Anger and Bargaining**: Anger in the stages of grief can manifest as frustration towards the world or specific individuals. In PTS and heightened anxiety, this anger might also be directed inwards, fueled by a sense of betrayal by one's own mind. The bargaining phase often involves "what if" scenarios, which, in the case of PTS and anxiety, can be rooted in deep-seated fears and a longing to return to a pre-trauma sense of self.

4. **Depression, Reflection, and Loneliness**: This stage involves a period of quiet reflection which can lead to feelings of depression and loneliness. For those with PTS and anxiety, these feelings are

often intertwined with a profound sense of loss – not just of what might have been but also of their own sense of self and security in the world.

5. **The Upward Turn**: As one begins to adjust to life with their condition, the intense feelings of pain and despair start to lift slightly. For individuals with PTS and heightened anxiety, this stage might also include a gradual rebuilding of confidence and a slow reclamation of their sense of self.

6. **Reconstruction and Working Through**: In this stage, individuals start to put the pieces of their life back together. This process can be more complex for those with PTS and anxiety, as it involves not only coming to terms with the past trauma but also overcoming the deep-rooted fears and confidence issues that have arisen as a result.

7. **Acceptance and Hope**: The final stage of grief is acceptance and looking forward. For those healing from PTS and anxiety, acceptance includes acknowledging and accepting their condition as a part of their life experience. It is also here that a renewed sense of self-confidence begins to emerge, fostering hope for the future.

The healing journey from PTS and heightened anxiety is a multifaceted process that encompasses the stages of grief, but with added layers of fear and loss of self-confidence. Understanding these stages and how they uniquely manifest in the context of trauma and anxiety can provide valuable insights for individuals navigating this path. It highlights the importance of a compassionate, patient approach to healing and the need for support systems that acknowledge the depth and complexity of this experience.

PART TWO with Jo -me

I certainly went through all 7 stages, and it was not consecutively, it was all over back and forth, in and out. Until, finally I was moving forward consistently, holding some level of steadiness day by day. That part was just as difficult as being full blown in grief and panic, as well as motivating to keep going. I could finally see glimmers of light at the end of tunnel. Like a candle that is struggling to stay lit while drowning in wet wax. Day by day I drained a bit of the wet wax to give the flickering flame room to breathe and grow. And it stayed small, but it stayed lit.

Let's start with number 1 Shock and denial. The Shock of the events was one thing, the denial of the impact was damaging and detrimental to say the least. I say this regarding the initial events and then the period of re-traumatization that occurred.

It was not only my denial of how affected I was, it was the denial of others or the avoidance to acknowledge how affected I was and how bad it was for me.

I can say this, there is a level of denial of how it impacts those close to you while you are drowning in the anxiety, fears, doubts and apprehensions. There just isn't room anywhere within you to see or feel outside of yourself. And that participates in number 2 Pain and Guilt.

For me this was huge, and in some ways, it contributed also to the heightened anxiety. I was someone who got through things, and someone who often felt for others more than myself. To experience the polar opposite of this brought discomfort at all levels. Guilt for causing pain to my husband, and or worry to those close to me. Guilt for some of the angry thoughts and words that rose to the surface without any filtering or awareness to the impact. Even looking back now I feel pangs of guilt for any hurt, that I so very much did not intend. It was always about being understood or desperate for relief and comfort of some kind. Those around me did not truly understand this. And in some ways, I don't think I did either

I am going to skip to number 4 Depression, Reflection, and Loneliness. This for me was the absolute worst part of the entire 3 some years. First off, I have never been depressed, experiencing this was brand new and horrible. I have been deeply sad but not depressed. And this kind of depression was devastating, dangerous and debilitating. With it came a loneliness I had never in my life felt.

Looking at this I feel the word "depression" may be overused and misused in our everyday language. Often, it's applied broadly to encompass a wide range of emotional experiences, diluting its true meaning and impact. I feel depression should not be a catch-all term for moments of sadness, stress, or temporary struggles. It is a singular, profoundly controlling condition that significantly affects one's mental, emotional, and physical well-being. Recognizing the severity and complexity of depression is crucial for ensuring it is taken seriously, respected, and treated with the appropriate level of care and understanding.

I say this from my heart on reflecting what I truly will acknowledge as depression that I experienced, and it is nothing like anything I'd ever felt in my life. And it wraps you in a straitjacket. That's the best way for me to think right now to explain that.

As I reflect on this chapter, I realize I very likely could write a second book on these 7 factors alone. Each and every one being a very large chapter. Every day forward has allowed me to get to a place of acceptance that it happened to me, and for forgiving myself for behaving the way I did, for feeling the way I did, for the thoughts I had, for the words I spoke. A lot that I just do not do. The entire experience is so far away from who I really am. Finding relief then acceptance has been a journey all on its own.

I believe that journey came form the old me scratching and clawing my way back to the surface or best said "out of the grave I was buried alive in."

Again, I say. Never Give Up!! One day the door just opens and lets you out to the light of day, the journey changes to something more meaningful and filled with hope.

11 Rediscovering Instinct: Navigating the Veil of PTS and Heightened Anxiety

In the shadow of Post-Traumatic Stress (PTS) and heightened anxiety, one of the most profound yet overlooked casualties is often our connection to instinct. This primal guide, which under normal circumstances serves as our internal compass, can become obscured or silenced amidst the turmoil. The "emotional volume" of fear, anxiety, and the constant attack of stress responses, not only mutes our instinctual cues but can also lead us to question them when they manage to break through. Here we explore the journey of losing touch with instinct due to PTS and heightened anxiety and offers insight into the path towards reclaiming this vital aspect of our being.

1. **The Muting of Instinct**: Under the influence of PTS and heightened anxiety, the mind is perpetually swamped with alarm signals, leaving little room for the subtle whispers of instinct. This constant state of vigilance shifts the focus towards immediate survival, often at the expense of the deeper, intuitive knowledge that guides us in making decisions aligned with our true selves. The result is a disconnection from an essential part of our identity and wisdom.

2. **Fear as the Dominant Emotional Volume**: Fear, a powerful and often overwhelming emotion, becomes the primary lens through which the individuals with PTS perceive the world. This heightened emotional volume can drown out the quieter, more nuanced signals of instinct. When fear dictates every decision, the space for instinctual guidance shrinks, making it challenging to discern which impulses are driven by immediate threats and which are informed by deeper, more meaningful insights.

3. **The Consequences of Disconnection**: Losing touch with one's instinct has profound implications. It can lead to feelings of

alienation from oneself, a sense of drifting without direction, and a disconnect from the very experiences that bring joy and fulfillment. Decisions become more challenging to make, as the internal compass that once offered certainty now seems unreliable or entirely silent.

4. **Pathways to Reconnection**: Reclaiming instinct amidst PTS and heightened anxiety is a gradual process that requires patience, awareness, and often, professional guidance. Mindfulness practices, such as meditation and focused breathing, can lower the "volume" of fear, allowing the quieter voice of instinct to emerge. Therapy can help individuals learn to differentiate between fear-driven reactions and genuine instinctual guidance.

5. **Cultivating a Safe Environment for Instinct**: Creating environments, both internally and externally, where instinct can thrive is crucial. Internally, this involves fostering a mindset of self-compassion and acceptance, where all emotions are acknowledged but do not hold absolute sway. Externally, surrounding oneself with supportive relationships and settings that encourage authenticity and exploration can reinforce the value of one's instinctual insights.

The journey to rediscover and trust in one's instinct while navigating the veils of PTS and heightened anxiety is both challenging and deeply rewarding. It involves understanding the mechanisms by which fear silences our deeper wisdom, and actively working towards creating a space where instinct can once again guide us. By doing so, we not only enhance our ability to navigate life more effectively but also reconnect with the most authentic parts of ourselves, paving the way for healing and true empowerment.

PART TWO with Jo -me

I very much relate to #3 The Consequences of Disconnection.

The line *"It can lead to feelings of alienation from oneself, a sense of drifting without direction, and a disconnect from the very experiences that bring joy and fulfillment."*

I relate to that, I felt all of that and then some. And sometimes now there moments of disconnection. They are very small. They're getting smaller and smaller and I'm thankful to be observing that. But I found it difficult to overcome and entirely frustrating to experience. Prior to my PTS I did not have any disconnection to my instinct, it was very strong, and I made life decisions based on my instinct, some of them life saving decisions.

As I have mentioned before or will likely mention again there is a "blankness" that occurred for me like holding two parts of myself in separate cages. The part of me that knows who am, who I have been and that is connected to my confidence was in a cage that is submerged and the messages from memories couldn't get through, it is warbly and unclear and weak from fighting fears doubts apprehensions. The part of me that was left frightened and locked in a cage had no idea what to do.

Today when I decided to add this section, I had been working on a topic in my Brewed Insights podcast about instinct. Ironically it set off in 3 different directions. And a realization of how much I had been disconnected to my instinct during those 3 years and how even now, I have moments where I pause and question, is this real, is this fear, is this a memory, is this my instinct?

Looking back at the memories I see some key areas where the instinctual part of me was trying to hold on, making me question circumstances and people, however in a different way than before. I would see something and see it as something that troubled me or made me uncomfortable, and sometimes totally freak out. I believe some of those moments were helpful to the situation, however I am not always clear how or why. And some contributed to the fear as I couldn't rectify the message.

For example, a man from a utility company came to my door, having no credentials, not wearing a mask during COVID before they opened it back up and wanting to come inside to turn the gas off, and I knew to say no, but I was numb and did not feel the entire situation, just the no.

This happened a lot. Looking at it now, I think perhaps the instinct was still there just getting confused by the way it had to get to the surface for me to notice, and then I simply did not know what to trust. A very difficult thing to experience for me, as in the past I had a strong connection to my instinct. Strong enough that I knew if someone was not a good person, and I was proven right many times.

As I write this it's Mar 11, 2024, I feel more connected to that part of me, however it is still somewhat muted or maybe it is that I am having a difficult time anchoring back into trusting it. Time will tell. Hopefully in a growing progress.

I came back to record this and today now is May 22, 2024. I will say that it feels like this part of me is coming back stronger and stronger everyday. I believe this connection is important to nurture and become aware of. Looking back, I can see many moments of either myself feeling something and looking but not realizing I was doing it. And some where ironically coming through others.

During the time we were renting the home we intended to heal, we hired a lovely man to help me with the gardens as there were a lot of them and quite a lot of work, and clearly there was a lot of labour and love was put into these gardens from the original owners who grew them. This man I will call G for privacy, he was one of the 16 individuals who I feel participated unknowingly in throwing me a lifeline to hold on to.

He took the time to have chats with me when he came to work, and these moments became very precious and actually important to me. For some reason, I trusted him, I don't know why but I did. I realize now that I did not even realize this, I felt safe to spend time with him, I am grateful for this more than he will ever know or could possibly understand.

During our chats he would randomly point out a hummingbird that came and hovered above us. Prior to my PTSD I loved hummingbirds and I felt they were visits from my mom who passed away, they always seemed to come when I was contemplating life in some way. Birds were my moms love. Anyway, when G would point them out, I remember turning and looking then feeling strangely blank yet feeling in the distance the subtle sound of 'awe, I love them'. That part is me, but it wasn't there, I couldn't connect that old self and the feeling.

Each time G pointed them out I felt them more and more, and I didn't realize it until now. Today I full on connect to that feeling again and I am grateful.

Number 4 Pathways to Reconnection and 5 Cultivating a Safe Environment for Instinct, I feel are interconnected. Having patience and awareness could not come unless I felt safe. In the small amounts of feeling safe and comfortable, being able to talk, laugh and smile gave me awareness in those small pockets of calm. I had these moments at times sitting out in the yard enjoying the sunshine and the quiet, when it was quiet. On these days a hummingbird always came.

Essentially it is a series of baby steps feeling more and more stable and secure. Hold onto the small moments you may not realize it, but they are very important in the journey back.

"Every morning, we are born again. What we do today is what matters most."

— *Buddha*

12 Moving Forward: Navigating Life After Experiencing PTS

Recovering from Post-Traumatic Stress (PTS) is a journey that requires patience, understanding, and a commitment to moving forward, despite the challenges. It's about finding balance, acknowledging your progress, and taking steps, however small, towards a future where you feel more in control and at peace. Some key points to consider when moving forward after experiencing PTS, focusing on the importance of routines, self-awareness, support systems, and allowing time for healing without the burden of expectations.

1. **Maintain or Establish Routines**: Routines can be a source of comfort and stability, especially in times of uncertainty and change. They provide a structure to your day, which can be particularly grounding when dealing with the unpredictability of PTS. If your old routines no longer fit your current situation, consider establishing new ones. This could involve setting regular times for meals, exercise, work, or relaxation. Routines don't have to be rigid; they should serve as a gentle framework to give your days a sense of normalcy and predictability.

2. **Notice How You're Feeling**: It's essential to regularly check in with yourself and notice how you're feeling. PTS can bring a range of emotions – from sadness and anger to hope and relief. Recognize and acknowledge these feelings without judgment. Understanding your emotional state is a crucial step in managing your symptoms and identifying what triggers may exacerbate your PTS.

3. **Find Safe and Supportive Networks**: Finding a support network where you feel safe to talk about your experiences and feelings is crucial. This support can come from friends, family, support groups, or mental health professionals. These networks provide a space to share your thoughts and feelings, offering you perspectives and

coping strategies that you might not have considered. Remember, seeking help is a sign of strength, not weakness.

4. **Allow Necessary Time Without Expectations**: Healing from PTS is not a linear process; it varies greatly from person to person. Allow yourself the time you need to heal without setting unrealistic expectations or timelines. Healing cannot be rushed. It's important to be patient with yourself and acknowledge that some days will be harder than others. Celebrate the small victories and understand that setbacks are also part of the journey.

5. **Engage in Activities That Bring Joy and Relaxation**: Engaging in activities that bring you joy, or relaxation can significantly aid in your recovery process. This might be hobbies like reading, painting, gardening, or simply spending time in nature. These activities not only provide a distraction from negative thoughts but also help in boosting your mood and overall sense of well-being.

6. **Practice Self-Compassion**: Be kind to yourself. Practicing self-compassion is vital in overcoming PTS. Speak to yourself with kindness and understanding, just as you would to a friend with a similar situation. Acknowledge your struggles and remind yourself of your resilience and the progress you've made.

Moving forward after experiencing PTS is a journey of self-discovery, resilience, and healing. It's about finding what works for you, whether it's maintaining routines, acknowledging your feelings, leaning on support systems, giving yourself time, engaging in joyful activities, or practicing self-compassion. Remember, every step forward, no matter how small, is progress on your path to recovery and well-being.

PART TWO with Jo -me

Moving forward with Little Hiccups

From Journaling Notes: June 3, 2024

June 2, A LADY WHO POKED THE BEAR -yesterday my husband and I were shopping and something made me notice a woman in the store we were in, she just felt off. It is funny because I recently was finishing multiple articles and a chapter about instinct, and here I was having one of those instinct moments.

She seemed to be hovering, watching but not watching and randomly viewing product. There are multiple factors to this particular situation that did not make sense. I did mention it to my husband when we left and were in our car, I felt she was either going to shoplift, a shoplifting security person or watching us. Everything about her was off, my husband somewhat agreed with my reasoning, and we left it at that.

Was it? Or wasn't it? I will never know. BUT it brought up the old feeling of being watched, that moved forward in this day, and I will say that incident may have been an emotional trigger that activated subconsciously and imposed itself throughout my day.

June 3, 2024: This morning I was making the bed and rolling random thoughts throughout my mind. I remember thinking to myself yesterday in my outburst of frustration "why, why am I feeling like this?" it took until today but I realized the chain of events yesterday that ultimately caused me to have a mini emotional blow up at dinner, were tied to feeling that lady was watching us/me, and though it didn't seem to bother me at the time, it clearly did subconsciously as it touched on the traumatic events of the past.

When standing in wet sand while ocean waves wash in and out on the shore, your feet sink, and the sand covers them up it is a continual movement of the grains of sand, but you move, and it ends. These moments of angst or frustration that arise are like standing still in the wet sand, if you don't move the grains will surround you and suck you down, into that wet sand deeper. Note to self; Feel those grains of sand coming in and covering you, MOVE, shift change the hidden feeling, it will be ok.

AH HA moments like this one, even not so positive can be beneficial. This one helped me see multiple ways I am still healing and growing from my PTS experience. It also showed me, that I am more connected again to my old self than I realized. Simply because I looked at that outburst and noticed, even if it was the next day, I noticed and that means I can shift the subconscious thinking to work for me not against me.

There will be more of these. I will get past each one. And now I can also ask is this from that or could I be tired, hungry? I definitely have had the hungry angry thing over the years. As I write this now, I am not sure what that mini outburst was. Looking at it, it feels like frustration more than a trigger, this is motivating.

I will be Ok!

Thank you, God/Universe, everything and everyone who participated in giving me anchors to hold to. And thank you to me, for grabbing on to those anchors. I am healing and back in control more and more every day!

Final Reflections

The Five Things That Saved Me and Kept me Trying

1. My husband's steadfast loyalty to me and supporting me.

Words escape me in attempting to articulate this, as there are so many parts regarding my husband during this horrible time for me. It was a horrible time for him also, and for the first time in our relationship I completely needed him more than I could give back.

At first, he didn't really know what to do, having never experienced me like this. I am sure inside; he was terrified of losing the women he fell in love with. I struggled to find in myself, something to say that would help him understand what I needed. I didn't even know what I needed, until one day I realized I needed to be held, I needed to be enveloped in his arms and heart so I could breathe, cry and breathe. I needed this over, and over again, and thankfully he did his best to realize when.

When I really had melt downs, and I mean melt downs! They were bursts of thoughts, feelings, emotions, fears, doubts, anger that could not be rectified on my own. I would yell all kinds of things; I would cry and dump the deepest darkest thoughts and feelings. Most times they were about myself, and what I felt was forever lost. He would respond with his deepest feelings of who I really am and never stopped telling me how strong I am, that I am stronger than most people, how good of person I was and how much he loved me. It may not have appeared to have helped often, but it helped to be supported in this way.

Don't get me wrong, we fought also, and these times were not kind by either of us, I will always have some form of guilt, most definitely sadness for this. I see him today and I know this journey gave him PTS also, and that just is not fare.

In the past in our relationship I was the optimist, he was a bit more of a pessimist in certain areas of life. During my worst PTS moments I was full on pessimist, I could not find the brighter side of anything. My husband stepped up! being in a dark place for himself also, and became stronger than ever before, holding on to us, and getting us through. He is really a good human, and an amazing partner that I am thankful and lucky to have.

2. Writing

From the very beginning I began writing out thoughts. They were all over and everywhere. About what happened, ideas about what it could have been, what people said around, how people acted anything that seemed to stand out. I would wake up around midnight in the beginning and write pages and pages. Dumping out of mind onto paper rather than in my sleep. I think this may have helped me still be able to sleep, one of things I didn't have to much trouble with, thankfully.

There is a mound of papers and journals from these 3 years of my life. I wrote more then, than perhaps in my entire life. I still do when a wave of feelings, thoughts, perspectives or questions occur, however it is smaller bits and wider timeframes than before. A sign of moving forward I suppose.

It is funny, in my work coaching, I understood the benefits of writing, particularly early mornings and evenings before bed. I also understood the dream cycles and how they are benefits to life and the minds wellbeing. I lost all awareness of this under the influence of heightened anxiety, subconsciously, interestingly, I helped myself through with this writing

The writing is why I began creating journals as I believe more in journaling than ever before.

3. One meditation audio

This today is still interesting to me. Previously I used my custom design of meditative hypnotherapy to work with clients. I created Zen 4 Minds a guided meditation site, for those out there in need that couldn't access one on one help. And I experienced seeing the benefits over the years working as a mind coach/mentor.

I could not meditate on my own, I could not use the tools I was trained to use. However, I found one guided meditation that I wrote, that was voiced by someone other than me, who has a beautiful voice and is a beautiful soul. This audio was the only one that I could listen to.

I think there are a couple of reasons, some I am still looking at deciphering, being a coach of course having a very deep understanding of the subconscious mind. The main reason during the darkest times was my mind could not share space with too many things, events, people etc. I was numb often, and if you gave me choice I could not decide. So subconsciously I assume I did what was best I chose one that simply worked and that was not me.

Not using names, however this person who voiced this meditation for Zen 4 Minds is a very good person. I know him to have a genuine kindness and spiritual depth I could relate to, and I admired. His voice is a beautiful tone that provided peaceful guidance to relax, let go and felt safe. Through my journey, feeling safe was the most important aspect of getting through. So, finding anything and everything that helped me feel safe in some capacity was key. I am very thankful and grateful for this audio this person voiced for me. Who knew?

4. Fur babies and new puppy companion!

OH MY GOD, I can not say enough how important my animals were. Animals just seem to know, they know when you need them, they know what to do and they give themselves selflessly to provide comfort.

In the beginning I had two cats and dog, the cats knew when to come and lie with me and simply purr. My dog Lucky was a rescue that had puppy PTS and to this day has anxiety that gives him a high arousal response at times. He was a lot of work however I was able to create a bond with him and help him feel safe with me, this took 3 years. He was 5ish when my PTS journey threw him into hyper protection mode from feeling me spiral into the darkest fearful energy. On one hand this made me feel safe and I NEEDED him around me always, sadly for him he too suffered the loss of me, in turn experiencing fears again, but he stayed loyal and strong for me. Both of us have softened now. Sometimes when we look at each other, it feels like he and I are reading each others' minds, there is a silent profound bond of trust between us that can not be broken.

Then came our second dog Paisley, her purpose was 3-fold, she was a mix of two breeds I had a fond love for from a dog I owned many years ago. The two breads are very strong in their minds and in protection. We felt she would be a good companion dog for my PTS, and focusing on training her may help my mind perhaps begin to have fun again. And my husband thought, a very special birthday present during a very horrible troublesome time, trying to bring me joy.

She was amazing to receive, and she did bring a level of "light" back to me. This was a year and half in my PTS and during a time where I was retraumatized by individuals void of human decency in an environment I should have felt safe in, that become one to use against me/us in deviously, cruel insensitive ways. Ironically, in the attempt to hurt me, using this new dog, they actually gave me something to stand up and fight for. Paisley gave me strength to live and fight for her! And here I am.

5. The memory of who I was before.

This is profoundly huge and small at the same time. Having a knowing that "before" I was strong, some would say fearless, however that wasn't entirely true. I just didn't like fear or feeling fear. I really didn't like it, so I would push through and find the solution that worked for me. I had always grown mentally emotionally very clear about life, thoughts, emotions, and perspectives, where I could very compassionately deal with most people and situations.

To lose access to this entirely was devastating and impossible to comprehend. It is in that impossible to comprehend, that kept the belief alive, flickering like a flame striving to stay lit. The old me, was still available inside somewhere. I tell you though it was locked in a cage, locked inside of a room with no windows and doors. And perhaps a few guard demons of negative thoughts to push me back for months and months and months.

When you can find memories of when you have been strong, they can throw anchors out into the abyss to give you enough strength to let those memories grow roots.

These 5 things are the only things that got me through. Well perhaps a few hummingbirds and ravens too, but that is another story about messages for later.

Something to realize this journey started in December 2020, I was retraumatized early 2021 through October 2022 that lingered with issues into 2023 and February 9, 2024, was the first day I said out loud to myself "I feel free"

Time is the journey, and it is your friend even when it does not feel to be. Have patience and understanding with yourself or those who you may know going through this type of journey.

Keys to the Cage

Perseverance

Endurance

Resilience

Courage

Healing

Strength

Clarity

Self-acceptance

Enlightenment

Growth

Empowerment

Hope

Why I Chose to Share My Journey

I suppose there will be a question to why I chose to share my journey. At some point I even questioned myself for a long time the thought of sharing my own story, my struggles and journey through Post-Traumatic Stress (PTS) and heightened anxiety, seemed unimaginable. The personal nature of these experiences often kept them shrouded in silence. However, as I navigated the turbulent waters of my own healing, I realized the profound impact that sharing could have – not just for me, but for others who might be on a similar path.

My experience with PTS did more than just challenge me; it provoked a deep desire to articulate this journey in a way that could offer comprehension, awareness, and understanding. I recognized that there are many out there, some in the midst of their struggles and others observing from the sidelines, trying to make sense of what's happening. My goal became clear: to provide insights and tools that could ease the journey for those battling heightened anxiety or PTS, and to offer a guiding light to those who stand by them. And quite honestly, knowing that this too would help me continue to heal and grow.

In pursuit of this goal, I created journals and a simple workbook designed to set daily intentions. These tools are intentionally brief and straightforward, minimizing resistance and making the process of introspection and goal setting as accessible as possible. I understand how overwhelming it can feel to face lengthy or complex tasks when dealing with anxiety, and I wanted to offer something that was easy to integrate into daily life.

Drawing from my background in working with individuals facing various challenges, I previously created Zen 4 Minds – a collection of meditations aimed at providing support and peace to those in need. These guided meditations are crafted to offer comfort and clarity, serving as a gentle companion in the journey towards healing or life in general. I am personally grateful to have created these meditations for others, ironically, one in general helped me in my journey with PTS

The impact of the COVID-19 pandemic, especially on children, further underscored the need for resources tailored to younger minds. Witnessing kids struggling more than ever, I was driven to create Zen 4 Little Ones. This series of bedtime meditative stories, specifically designed for children, helping them find calm, let go of stresses of the day and in a world that has become increasingly uncertain and difficult for their young minds to navigate.

Ultimately, my journey through PTS and the creation of these resources, is rooted in a deep-seated desire to help. It's about extending a hand, sharing insights, and providing practical tools to those navigating on similar paths. By opening about my experience and offering these resources, I hope to foster a sense of understanding, connection, and, most importantly, hope.

Closing Thoughts

Who I Was, Who I am Now, Embracing Hope and Life

I have mentioned multiple times that before I was generally calm, comfortable and confident. Someone that others often were drawn to for support and acknowledgment. I was successful in meeting others in a non-judgmental way. It is still uncomfortable to know that I lost myself in so many ways during this turbulent 3+ years. It is uncomfortable putting the pieces of my life back together, particularly feeling that my life my career, my passion, were torn to shreds, and here I am at the age of 58 starting over in so many ways.

I am starting over; this is very clear. The new me is going to come out even stronger than before. I can feel this in my heart. And in the pit of my stomach, I feel the seed of determination bursting into bloom just like Spring.

So many parts of me from the old self will be wiser, and even more worldly than before. I used to say I am ok with "the stories of my past" that others felt were traumatic, they all made me who I am. They made me strong. I can still say this and feel that I will be ok and proud of who I am after this traumatic event that was truly traumatizing. However, one thing will be different, I am not sure that I can justify forgiveness for complete assholes anymore. I used to be able to try and see the others perspective, at this time, this has changed when it comes to self serving people. Time will tell, I guess.

I came across this quote recently, that now is placed on my wall with intentions of reminding me daily.

"Nothing is impossible, the word itself says I'm possible!"

~ Audrey Hepburn

There is a sentence I have used often within my work as Hypnotherapist/Mind Coach and in my guided meditations that ironically is fitting to use in closing:

"allow yourself to let go of thoughts and **experience** relaxing....."

"There is no right way, there is no wrong way"

Thank You

Thank you for embarking on this journey with me. Here's to a life lived with purpose, joy, and unwavering hope.

I'm Jo and this is the beginning of a new story.............

Warmly,
Jo Harris

Thank You and Acknowledgement

To maintain privacy, I wish to extend my deep, sincere gratitude to several individuals, including my family, who have supported me through the three-plus years of my PTSD. There were many days when I teetered on the edge of the cliff, and each of you provided me with something to hold on to, pulling me back to stable ground time and time again.

During a period of sheer terror and deep-seated fear, when I didn't know whom, I could trust or if I was safe, each of you offered me a lifeline back to myself in some way. Thank you for gifting me hope. I am eternally grateful.

D - my partner, husband, friend, my light, and my other reason to be committed to healing. You are so strong. You pulled me off the cliff over and over and over, I love you! I know I was your rock and to have fallen apart must have been excruciating for you emotionally while trying to hold things together let alone work to provide for our family. You will never fully understand the thousands of moments when I saw how much you were struggling to stay supportive and how "the steady Eddie" in you stayed true to the heart and stood by me the very best you could. The little moments where the old me' could remind the current me to look and listen to who I am and gave me hope that I would survive and be ok. The many times you reminded me "I am not weak I am strong". The many times you told me you loved me or just simply held my hand. 16 years in and life came right off the rails. You are a mountain in my life that I trust and am deeply grateful for the unmoveable support and love you give me. Now at 19 years and hopefully a few more lifetimes. May our souls always find each other.

I LOVE YOU! ∞ ∞ ∞ ∞ ∞ ∞

My son "Buddy" my beautiful boy, who turned out to be a beautiful man! Thank you for helping us during a horrible time with honour, grace, and selflessly during a time that was difficult for you as well. I am proud to be your mom, I am proud of who you are! I can not imagine how hard it may have been to navigate me or to find the energy to figure out how to help.

I LOVE YOU! ∞ ∞ ∞ ∞ ∞ ∞

16 INDIVIDUALS Including my fur babies & Rosie, someone else's fur baby. All beacons of light each one individually gave me strength and an anchor to hold on to. None were less or more significant.

My clients – each and every one! For over 14 years you trusted me with your story, your thoughts, and your feelings. I am grateful, honored to have been able to help you in your individual journeys. Having listened to your stories there is an ironic synchronicity that helped me through my darkest time. Having heard the pain some of you were going through and watching you strive to overcome, seeing so many of you grow and move through, gave me strong reminders subconsciously of strength and endurance. In essence, your stories and your success helped me too.

Blessings to all of you. I am grateful!

"Kindness is a language
which the deaf can hear
and the blind can see." -

MARK TWAIN

About the Author

Jo Harris is an entrepreneur, writer, mind coach, and certified hypnotherapist. She is a mom, wife, and passionate animal lover, who finds joy in laughing out loud, and living life with awareness and compassion.

In 2008 she stepped out of the corporate world to start her own practice "Coaching 4 Minds" and began working with clients as a mind coach/hypnotherapist offering insights, support, and perspectives about life, relationships, personal growth, psychology, spirituality, and self-awareness. Before that, Jo spent many years in Senior Management in Retail, Tech, and Hospitality.

She is the creator of Zen 4 Minds Guided Meditations, Zen 4 Little One's Meditative Bedtime Stories, Jot the Thought-Zen 4 Minds Journaling, notebooks and journals, and CEO of Jot The Thought Media Ltd.

Her coined philosophy "Live Like a Zen Puppy" is her life motto to live by. ZEN suggests being peaceful and relaxed. PUPPY suggests being happy, fun, full of life. Everyone wishes to find more peace and be relaxed, and everyone wants to be happy and have fun in life. Live Like a Zen Puppy is a concept of having both and helping others to find/have both too!

Further Credit

Invaluable assistance provided by ChatGPT, an AI developed by OpenAI, for insightful suggestions and support in the creation of this book

Though my intention was to write this book without help, I discovered two key areas that caused me to pause with either difficulty or discomfort.

Discomfort came from attempting to create a bio about myself simply from still feeling punches to my self esteem from the PTSD. The difficulty came at times while writing the introduction, putting my idea into words was a collaboration of my thoughts and ChatGPT's ability to articulate my design.

Thanks Chat!

Author's Note

Writing this book has been a journey filled with tears, sweat, and profound healing. My intention in sharing this story was not only to expand awareness and help others but also to release my own demons. Each page is a testament to the struggles and triumphs experienced along the way.

I hope that through these words, you find comfort, insight, and a sense of connection. Your support means the world to me, and if this book has touched you in any way, I would be deeply grateful if you could share your thoughts through a review. Your feedback helps others find this book and continue their own journeys of healing and self-discovery.

You may leave a review at https://www.anxietymindsetdiaries.com/review/

Thank you for joining me on this path.

Warmly,

Jo Harris

Additional Resources by Jo

Thank you for reading "Anxiety Mindset Diaries" I hope you found it insightful and empowering. To continue your journey and explore more resources, visit the following links:

The Mindsets Space with Jo Harris

- **Website:** https://joharris.blog The Mindsets Space

- **Guided Meditations**: Explore a wide range of guided meditations designed to help you reframe subconscious patterns, overcome fears and anxieties, and discover new perspectives on life.

- **Community**: Join our supportive community to connect with like-minded individuals and share your journey.

- **Blog**: Read articles covering diverse topics to educate, inspire, and foster community support.

- **Memberships**: Join the "Mindsets Space Group" for exclusive content and resources.

Zen for Minds

- **Website:** https://zenforminds.com Zen for Minds or join the mindset space https://joharris.blog for old and new guided meditations

- **Subscription Service**: Access exclusive guided meditations to support your mental well-being and personal growth.

Brewed Insight Podcast

- **Listen Here:** https://joharris.blog, Spotify, Apple and Amazon Music

- **Episodes**: Dive into engaging discussions on various topics, including 'The Overuse of Positive Thinking' and 'High Functioning or High Avoidance.'

Zen 4 Little One's – Children's Meditative Bedtime stories

- **Website**: https://zen4littleones.com Zen 4 Little Ones

- **Children's Meditative Bedtime stories:** where children embark on enchanting & magical journeys. These meditation bedtime stories are intricately crafted meditative mind moments that gently cradle young minds, helping them release the day's fears, anxieties, and stress.

Anxiety Harmony Community

- **Join Here**: https://joharris.blog Anxiety Harmony Community

- **Don't Let Go:** Ongoing dialogue from the book, straight talk about anxiety, heightened anxiety and PTSD and more.

- **Support**: Share and support each other through anxiety in our dedicated forum.

Social Media

- **Facebook**: Mindsets Space with Jo Harris

- **X (Twitter):** Mindsets Space with Jo Harris

- **Instagram**: @themindsetsspace

For more information, updates, and resources, please visit our websites and follow us on social media. Thank you for being a part of this journey. Together, we can create a world of possibilities.

The world needs more sensitive perspectives that move others to make things better!